Content

Introduction
Becoming a Master Strategist

Part 1
Becoming the Unthinkable: Breaking the Boundaries of Ordinary Thinking
   Chapter 1 :Belief :The Invisible Hand of Beliefs
   Chapter 2: Rethinking : Breaking the Mental Mold
   Chapter 3: Failure as Success: The Art of Falling Forward
   Chapter 4: Habits: They are Secondary

Part 2
Foresight: Seeing Beyond The Present Trade
   Chapter 5: The Brain: A Predicting Machine
   Chapter 6: Thinking in Scenarios : Crafting future possibilities
   Chapter 7: Mastery in Planning: The Blueprint for Trading Success

Part 3
The Strategist's Blueprint : Mastering the Foundation of Insights
   Chapter 8: History: The Key
   Chapter 9: Mastering One Asset: The Power of Focus
   Chapter 10: The Strategy: Building the Blueprint

Part 4
The Training Grounds: Where Mastery is Forged
   Chapter 10: The Silent Weapon: The Mind Needs Rest
   Chapter 11: The Four Stages of Development: From Novice To Mastery in Trading
   Chapter 12: Mastering the Craft: Developing Skills Through

Consistent, Focused Practice

Part 5
Beyond profits: Seeing the Big Picture
  Chapter 13: Three Months, Not One Trade: The Long Game
  Chapter 14: The checklist: Turning Complexity into Simplicity
  Chapter 15: The Shadow Mentor:Coaching Yourself from the Third Perspective

Part 6
The Lazy Couch: Strategic Rest
  Chapter 16: The Silent Weapon: The Mind Needs Rest
  Chapter 17: The Aha Moment: Clarity in Stillness
  Chapter 18: The currency of energy: Being Intentional with Time

Conclusion
The Journey Mastery

Introduction: Becoming a Master Strategist

Trading is more than numbers on a screen or patterns on a chart, it's a mind game, a battle of discipline, and a test of strategic thinking. Every decision, every trade, every moment of hesitation is part of a larger narrative that shapes your journey as a trader. To become truly successful, you must move beyond the technicalities and embrace the art of strategy. This book is about becoming a master strategist in the unpredictable world of trading.

A master strategist doesn't just react to market movements, they anticipate, plan, and execute with precision. They know that success isn't about winning every trade but about developing a system that thrives over the long term. They see beyond the momentary fluctuations and think in terms of cycles, trends, and probabilities. More importantly, they understand that trading is not just a skill but a mindset, one that requires mastery over emotions, discipline, and the ability to see the bigger picture.

But becoming a master strategist isn't easy. It requires more than technical knowledge; it demands that you reshape how you think, feel, and act in the face of uncertainty. This journey is about learning to control your impulses, trust the process, and consistently make calculated decisions, even when emotions are pulling you in the opposite direction.

In this book, we will go beyond traditional trading advice. Together, we'll explore how your beliefs shape your success, how failure can be a powerful tool for growth, and how to think in scenarios rather than single outcomes. You'll learn to develop a mindset that transcends short-term profits and focuses on building a sustainable, long-term strategy.

As you read, you'll discover that the most powerful tools a trader has aren't found in market indicators but in their ability to manage themselves. This is your playbook for becoming a master strategist, for seeing the market as a battlefield where the sharpest weapon is your mind, and your greatest ally is the ability to stay ahead by thinking, adapting, and evolving.

This book will challenge you to rethink your approach, to see trading not as a quick game of chance, but as a profound strategic pursuit. Through these pages, you'll learn the key principles and insights that will help you transform from a trader into a strategist, one who isn't just playing the game, but mastering it.

Part 1

Becoming the Unthinkable : Breaking the Boundaries of Ordinary Thinking

In trading, true masters stand apart as visionaries navigating the market's unseen currents. Becoming the unthinkable means shattering conventional beliefs that limit your potential.

This journey begins with awakening to the barriers your assumptions create. By viewing failure as a catalyst for growth, you'll transform setbacks into opportunities.

Embrace the mindset of a strategist, redefine your relationship with risk, cultivate resilience, and welcome discomfort. Each challenge is a chance to evolve, paving the way to becoming a trader who commands the market amidst uncertainty.

Chapter 1

Beliefs: The invisible hand

Beliefs. They are invisible forces that drive every decision you make, every risk you take, and every reward you seek. In the world of trading, beliefs are both your greatest asset and your most dangerous liability. What you believe shapes how you see the market, how you interpret its movements, and ultimately, how you act. The master strategist understands this and actively works to reshape beliefs to align with long-term success.

But here's the trap: beliefs can also misguide you. They can trick you into seeing patterns where none exist, into trusting strategies that are flawed, or into holding on to losing trades long after logic has told you to walk away. This chapter will dive deep into the profound impact beliefs have on your trading and how mastering them is the first step toward becoming a true strategist.

How beliefs shape your trading

Every trader has beliefs about the market, whether conscious or unconscious. You may believe that the market is predictable, or that success comes from gut instincts, or that technical analysis is the holy grail. These beliefs form the foundation of your trading decisions. They dictate whether you're a risk-taker or risk-averse, a day trader or a long-term investor, an emotional trader or a methodical one.

Beliefs create your reality in the market.

When you believe something to be true, your mind subconsciously searches for evidence to support it. For example, if you believe the market is rigged, you'll notice every trade that goes against you as proof. If you believe in a certain strategy, you'll see every success as validation, even if it was just luck. This cognitive bias, called *confirmation bias*, can lock you into a specific way of thinking, which becomes dangerous in the ever-evolving world of trading.

Beliefs shape your perception

Imagine two traders looking at the same chart. One sees a buying opportunity, the other sees a warning sign. Why? Because their beliefs are different. One may believe in momentum trading, while the other believes in contrarian strategies. Their beliefs act as filters, determining what they notice and what they ignore.

As a trader, you must recognize that your beliefs act as lenses through which you view the market. If your beliefs are aligned with reality, they'll guide you toward profitable decisions

But if they're distorted or outdated, they'll lead you into traps. For instance, if you believe that the market always bounces back after a dip, you may hold on to losing trades longer than you should, waiting for the reversal that never comes. Or, if you believe that you need to be right all the time to succeed, you'll struggle with cutting your losses, because every loss feels like a personal failure rather than a necessary part of the process.

The trap of fixed beliefs

The most dangerous aspect of beliefs in trading is their ability to become fixed. When beliefs solidify into certainties, they become mental traps. Traders who fall into these traps become rigid, unwilling to adapt or evolve with the market. This rigidity is a death sentence in an environment that rewards flexibility and adaptability.

Take the trader who believes that a specific indicator is foolproof. They trust it so completely that they ignore all other signals. They follow the indicator even when the market conditions have changed, and as a result, they lose money. This is the trap of over-reliance on fixed beliefs.

Markets are fluid. They change, evolve, and sometimes behave irrationally. A belief that worked for years can suddenly become irrelevant. If you're too attached to that belief, you'll be blindsided when the market shifts, and you'll find yourself holding on to a strategy that no longer works.

The master strategist recognizes that beliefs must be flexible. Success in trading requires constant questioning, testing, and rethinking. Fixed beliefs will lead you down the same paths over and over again, even when those paths no longer lead to profits.

The influence of beliefs on trading psychology

Beliefs are powerful because they aren't just intellectual ideas—they're emotional drivers. A trader's beliefs about money, risk, and success are deeply rooted in their psychology. These emotional beliefs can misguide you in ways that logic and reason can't.

For example, if you believe that losing money is a reflection of your worth as a trader, you'll be paralyzed by fear when the market moves against you. You'll hesitate to take trades because the potential for loss feels too personal. On the other hand, if you believe that success in trading is purely about winning big, you'll take on too much risk, chasing after the adrenaline rush of massive profits.

Both of these emotional beliefs are misguided. Trading is not about winning or losing on a personal level, it's about executing a strategy over time. But when your beliefs are tied to your emotions, every trade becomes a high-stakes event that's filled with pressure, fear, and greed.

This emotional misguidance can be disastrous. It leads to revenge trading after a loss, overconfidence after a win, and hesitation when you should be taking action. The master strategist works to separate their emotional beliefs from their trading decisions, knowing that emotions cloud judgment and distort reality.

Challenging and eveloving your beliefs

To become a master strategist, you must learn to constantly challenge your beliefs. This isn't easy. It requires humility, self-awareness, and a willingness to admit that you might be wrong. But it's essential for long-term success.

The market is always changing, and as it does, your beliefs need to evolve with it. What worked in a bull market might not work in a bear market. The indicators you relied on a year ago might not be as reliable today. The strategies that brought you profits in the past might no longer be effective. If you cling to your old beliefs, you'll find yourself stuck in outdated patterns, unable to adapt to new opportunities.

Rethinking is a critical skill in trading.It's the ability to step back, question your assumptions, and adjust your beliefs based on new information. The master strategist regularly reviews their beliefs, asking tough questions:

- Is this belief still serving me?
- Is there evidence that contradicts this belief?
- How might this belief be limiting my success?

By challenging and evolving your beliefs, you keep yourself open to new ideas and new strategies. You become more flexible, more adaptive, and more capable of thriving in any market condition.

A framework for success

So, how do you build beliefs that guide you toward success rather than lead you into Traps? It starts with **awareness**. You must become conscious of the beliefs that are driving your decisions. Often, these beliefs are so ingrained that you don't even realize they're there.

Take some time to reflect on the following questions:

- What do I believe about the market?
- What do I believe about risk?
- What do I believe about my ability to succeed in trading?

Once you've identified your core beliefs, examine them critically. Are they based on evidence? Are they helping you or holding you back? Beliefs should be grounded in reality, not in hope or fear.

The next step is to replace limiting beliefs with empowering ones. If you believe that you need to be right all the time, replace that belief with the understanding that losses are a natural part of trading. If you believe that the market is unpredictable and chaotic, replace that with the belief that while you can't control the market, you can control your actions within it.

Beliefs that support long-term success are flexible, grounded, and aligned with the reality of the market. They allow you to adapt to changing conditions, manage your emotions, and stay focused on your strategy rather than getting caught up in the short-term noise.

The Belief System of a Master Strategist

At the core of every successful trader is a belief system that supports their growth, adaptability, and resilience. Beliefs shape your reality in the market, but they can also trap you in cycles of failure if they're misguided or outdated.

The master strategist doesn't take their beliefs for granted. They challenge them, test them, and evolve them over time. They recognize that beliefs are not fixed, and that success in trading requires constant rethinking and refinement.

As you move forward in your trading journey, take the time to examine your beliefs. Understand how they're shaping your decisions, how they might be trapping you, and how they can be misguiding you. And most importantly, be willing to evolve those beliefs as you grow. In doing so, you'll not only become a better trader, you'll become a true master strategist.

Chapter 2
Rethinking: Breaking the mental mold

In trading, the most powerful tool isn't your strategy, it's your mind. Yet, many traders unknowingly trap themselves in mental molds built from past wins and ingrained beliefs. What if the very ideas that once brought success are now holding you back? To master the market, you must master the art of rethinking.

Rethinking isn't about admitting you're wrong, it's about questioning your assumptions even when you're right. The market evolves, and so must your approach. The traders who rise above don't cling to old patterns, they adapt by constantly challenging their own perspectives.

Imagine a path that changes with every step. Those who succeed don't follow old maps, they redraw them. Rethinking allows you to see beyond your biases, spot new opportunities, and keep evolving. In this chapter, we'll explore how to deconstruct outdated beliefs and build a mindset that thrives on change, unlocking your full potential as a strategist.

The power of perception

You control what you see. You can make it either good or bad. Your perception is your reality, but where does that reality begin? What you see stems from your beliefs. Those beliefs shape how you interpret everything, from the markets to your daily life. But beliefs are not concrete truths; they are stories we tell ourselves based on our experiences, our fears, and our expectations.

So, where do these beliefs come from? They all start from a single thought, a small, fleeting idea that often slips into your mind and vanishes as quickly as it appeared. Most of the time, these thoughts pass through without leaving a trace, but every now and then, one sticks. It grows, gains momentum, and eventually becomes a belief. Like a seed, once planted, it influences the way you see the world.

In trading, this can be dangerous. One bad trade can give birth to a belief that you're a poor trader, or that the market is against you. These beliefs, rooted in fear or frustration, can cloud your judgment. They may cause you to act on emotions rather than logic. The antidote to this? The ability to rethink.

The silent virus

Thoughts are like viruses. They arrive quietly, unnoticed, and for a time, they seem harmless. Just like how a cold virus enters your body without immediate symptoms, a thought can settle into your mind without you realizing its potential impact. Days or weeks may go by, and then, suddenly, you're overwhelmed. The thought has grown into something much bigger, a belief that influences your actions and shapes your reality.

When a virus takes over your body, you feel drained, weak, and off balance. Similarly, a harmful belief can distort your trading decisions. It clouds your vision and makes you react impulsively. The market no longer appears neutral; instead, it becomes a battlefield of emotions where every price movement feels like a personal attack. Your belief in your ability to trade effectively erodes, and with it, your performance declines.

But just as the body can heal with the right antidote, your mind can recover with the antidote of rethinking. To rethink is to challenge those beliefs that were born from passing thoughts. It's the process of identifying what's real and what's merely a mental construct. You begin to see the market for what it is, an impartial system, not an enemy. You start to reclaim control, not just over your trades but over your mind.

The art of rethinking

Rethinking is an art. It requires stepping back from the immediate noise of the market and looking at your own internal landscape. What stories are you telling yourself about your trading? Are these stories serving you, or are they sabotaging you? The first step is awareness. Acknowledge that your beliefs shape how you perceive everything, including the financial markets. But more importantly, recognize that you have the power to change those beliefs.

The key to rethinking is curiosity. Instead of rigidly holding onto a belief, ask yourself questions. "Why do I believe this?" "Where did this belief come from?" "Is it based on facts, or is it an emotional reaction?" This habit of questioning your beliefs opens the door to change. It allows you to see beyond the limitations of your current mindset and explore new possibilities.

In trading, this could mean questioning the belief that a loss defines you as a trader. Maybe you've held onto a losing position too long, believing it will turn around, not because the market data supports it, but because you're the market data supports it, but because you're emotionally attached to the trade. Rethinking helps you see that the belief is flawed, and you can release it before more damage is done.

From belief to action

Once you've identified a belief that's holding you back, what do you do with it? It's not enough to simply recognize it; you have to replace it with something better. Rethinking is about rewiring your thought patterns. You must take conscious action to install new, empowering beliefs that serve your goals.

For example, instead of believing that you have to win every trade to be successful, shift your belief to this: "Every trade is a learning opportunity." This change in belief doesn't just alter your mindset; it transforms your behavior. You stop chasing perfection and start focusing on process and progress.

New beliefs lead to new actions. In trading, this might mean implementing better risk management strategies, being more patient with entries, or being quicker to cut losses. Your mindset becomes your greatest asset, and rethinking is the tool that sharpens it.

cleansing the mind

Beliefs are deeply intertwined with emotions, and many of our most deeply held beliefs come from emotional experiences. This is why rethinking often requires emotional detoxification. You have to clear the emotional residue that has built up from past experiences, such as fear from past losses or excitement from short-lived wins.

Rethinking isn't just about intellectual analysis, it's also about emotional release. As you confront and challenge limiting beliefs, emotions will rise to the surface. Let them. It's important to feel and process them rather than suppress them. Emotional freedom leads to mental clarity, and with that clarity, you can begin to see the market with fresh eyes.

In trading, emotional detox might mean revisiting a trade that went wrong and understanding the emotions that drove your decisions. Maybe it was fear of missing out that caused you to enter too early, or panic that made you sell too late. By acknowledging these emotions and letting go of the belief that they have power over you, you regain control.

Build Resilience Through Rethinking

Resilience is a byproduct of rethinking. As you challenge and reshape your beliefs, you become more adaptable. You realize that no matter what happens in the market, you have the capacity to respond thoughtfully, not reactively. This mental flexibility is crucial in a world as unpredictable as trading.

Beliefs that once trapped you in cycles of self-doubt or fear lose their grip. You start to trust in your ability to navigate the market, not because you expect every trade to be a win, but because you know that you can learn from every outcome. With rethinking, failure becomes feedback, and uncertainty becomes opportunity.

Rethinking strengthens the mind just as physical exercise strengthens the body. It trains you to stay composed in volatile markets, to adapt to unexpected events, and to maintain a long-term perspective even in the face of short-term losses. Over time, rethinking becomes your natural response to challenges, and with it, resilience becomes your foundation.

Rethinking as a Daily Practice

Rethinking is not a one-time event; it's a daily practice. Just as you analyze the markets each day, you must analyze your own thoughts. Begin every trading day with a mental check-in. Ask yourself: "What beliefs am I bringing into today's market? Are they helping me, or hindering me?" By consciously rethinking each day, you prevent harmful beliefs from taking root.

Make rethinking part of your routine, like checking your charts or reviewing your trades. Reflect on your day's actions and decisions, and ask yourself where your beliefs might have influenced your behavior. Did you hesitate to enter a winning trade because of fear? Did you hold onto a losing trade too long out of hope? Identifying these patterns allows you to rethink them before they become ingrained.

The Power of a Rethought Mind

Imagine the trader you can become when rethinking is second nature. A mind that is constantly evolving, questioning, and reshaping itself is one that can thrive in any market. You will no longer be shackled by limiting beliefs or emotional reactions. Instead, you will approach trading with a sense of clarity and confidence that comes from knowing you have the power to control not just your trades but your mind.

As you continue to rethink, you will realize that the market is not a place of chaos but a place of endless possibilities. And you, with a mind that is free from the viruses of limiting beliefs, are perfectly equipped to seize those possibilities. In trading, as in life, rethinking is the key to transformation.

Chapter 3

Failure as success : The Art of Falling Forward

What if failure isn't the end, but a stepping stone? What if failure is the exact tool that sharpens your edge, preparing you for the next battle? The truth is, failure in trading, or in life is inevitable. Yet, so many view it as an endpoint, a wall that stops them from moving forward. But a strategist knows better. Failure is not the enemy; it is the guide that points you toward success.

Redefining failure

In trading, losses are often interpreted emotionally, frustration, disappointment, and sometimes even self-doubt creep in. But what if you paused, rethought your position, and stepped back from that emotional turmoil? Within every failure, there lies an opportunity, waiting to be discovered. Failure gives you data. It shows you what didn't work, what requires improvement, and where your blind spots lie. In the trading world, this insight is invaluable. Each misstep presents a lesson, and when examined thoughtfully, it becomes a tool to refine your strategy.

Markets, as we know, don't care about our wins or losses. They are neutral forces moving with or without us. But as a master strategist, you have the unique power to extract value from each trade, even the ones that didn't go your way. The key is in shifting your mindset: see failure as a mentor, not an enemy. With this redefined perspective, failure becomes a mirror, reflecting areas that demand growth, enabling you to make informed adjustments.

Success is built on layers of failure, but only if you allow yourself to grow from those experiences. A loss isn't a verdict on your capabilities as a trader; it's an invitation to rethink your approach, fine-tune your skills, and come back stronger.

The Anatomy of a Setback

On the surface, a failure in trading might seem straightforward: a trade didn't go your way, your prediction was wrong, or your strategy faltered. However, every failure has multiple layers. There is more beneath the surface than a simple mistake; each setback contains vital clues about mindset, risk tolerance, and trading discipline.

A losing trade may appear to be the result of an incorrectly timed entry or misinterpreted market signals. But peel back the layers, and you may uncover deeper issues: overconfidence, impulsiveness, or even fear. For example, overconfidence might drive a trader to assume the market will align with their will, dismissing signals that caution against entering a trade. Similarly, fear might cause hesitation, leading to missed opportunities or poor exits. These mistakes aren't just about execution—they're reflections of your mental state during the trade.

Failures are not just hiccups along your journey. Each setback is an opportunity to dissect your actions, your emotions, and your decision-making processes. A failure reveals your psychological makeup under pressure, your level of discipline, and your ability to manage risk. When approached with curiosity and humility, the analysis of failures offers invaluable lessons, which become tools in your evolution as a trader.

The difference between successful and unsuccessful traders lies in how they handle these moments. While some view failures as obstacles, others see them as openings for learning. The strategic mind embraces failure as a teacher, recognizing that within every loss lies the roadmap to future success.

Turning losses into leverage

The true art of mastering failure comes when you learn to turn it into leverage. A loss is not simply a loss, it's potential energy waiting to be harnessed. The difference between a novice trader and a master strategist is how they respond to losses. A novice is often paralyzed by failure, while a master strategist uses it as leverage to push forward, refine their strategy, and ultimately improve.

Turning failure into leverage requires a shift in mindset. First, you must adopt a broader perspective. Zoom out, and see the bigger picture. One loss doesn't define your career; it's merely one point on a much larger continuum. When you examine your losses in the context of your overall journey, you start to see patterns and areas where growth is needed.

Beyond perspective, the key to turning losses into leverage is to develop a process of reflection. After every trade, win or lose take the time to review what happened. What worked? What didn't? More importantly, why didn't it work? This process of reflective review ensures that every loss becomes a learning experience, something you can extract value from.

Implementing this process requires a shift in your routine. Just as you would review charts or analyze data, reviewing your mindset and behavior after a trade becomes a crucial part of your strategy. Did you act out of emotion? Were you patient with your analysis? Was your risk management sound? Each of these questions becomes part of your framework for turning losses into leverage.

The market rewards those who adapt and grow. By leveraging your losses, you position yourself to evolve, developing resilience and insight. Every time you turn a loss into leverage, you strengthen the foundation of your strategic mind, and soon, what seemed like a failure becomes part of your ultimate success.

The Emotional Weight of Failure

Failure isn't just about the numbers on a screen. It's about how those numbers make you feel. The emotional weight of failure can be overwhelming, especially when the stakes are high. In trading, where the outcome of a decision can impact financial stability, emotions like fear, frustration, and even shame can cloud your judgment.

But as a master strategist, part of your growth involves learning to manage these emotions. Trading is not just a test of technical skill; it's a test of emotional resilience. How you handle the emotional fallout of failure determines whether that failure will fuel your growth or drag you down.

Recognizing the emotional weight of failure is the first step. The next is learning how to release it. That's where rethinking comes in. The ability to step back and evaluate your emotional reactions gives you the power to break free from the grip of negative emotions. You stop seeing failure as a personal flaw and start viewing it as an essential part of the learning process.

Every time you overcome the emotional weight of failure, you build mental toughness. You learn to face losses with clarity rather than fear, and that resilience becomes your greatest asset in the volatile world of trading.

Build resilence through failure

Resilience is the natural byproduct of facing failure head-on. Every time you fall and get back up, you build a layer of strength, both mentally and emotionally. As a trader, resilience is your secret weapon. It's what keeps you in the game when others are bowing out, discouraged by losses.

Failure teaches you flexibility. It shows you that no matter how well you prepare, no trade is guaranteed. But rather than becoming disillusioned, the master strategist uses this knowledge to build resilience. You become adaptable, learning to shift strategies quickly when the market demands it. You realize that every setback is an opportunity to pivot, to rethink your approach, and to grow.

In trading, as in life, resilience is key to longevity. The market will test you—there's no avoiding that. But with each failure, you gain more insight, more strength, and more wisdom. And over time, your resilience becomes the bedrock of your trading strategy.

Failure as a Catalyst for Success

The most successful traders aren't the ones who avoid failure; they are the ones who embrace it. Failure is not a detour; it's part of the road. Each failure brings you closer to success because each one teaches you something you didn't know before. The key is to approach failure not with dread but with curiosity.

As a master strategist, you don't just survive failure, you thrive on it. You use it as a catalyst for success, understanding that every loss, every setback, every moment of doubt is an opportunity to rethink, to recalibrate, and to come back stronger.

In the world of trading, success is not about never failing; it's about how you rise from those failures. It's about turning each setback into a stepping stone, leveraging your losses to fuel your progress. The path to mastery is paved with failures, but with each one, you are shaping yourself into a more resilient, more strategic trader.

Failure isn't the opposite of success, it's the precursor to it.

Chapter 4

Habits: They are Secondary

Habits shape the rhythm of our lives. They guide us through our routines, structuring our days and organizing our actions into familiar patterns. But here's the often overlooked truth—while habits are powerful, they are not the ultimate force behind success. In trading, habits are secondary to something far more essential: the mind's ability to rethink, adapt, and evolve.

Traders are often obsessed with creating the "perfect" habit—whether it's a foolproof morning routine, a reliable trading system, or an unbreakable schedule. But even the most disciplined habits can become traps if they're followed without the flexibility to adapt. Habits without a resilient, adaptable mind behind them are like a beautifully constructed house without a solid foundation—appealing on the surface, but unstable when the ground shifts.

Success in trading comes not from perfect habits but from the ability to adjust those habits when necessary. The real power lies in the mind's capacity to evolve, rethink, and adapt. Habits may guide your process, but the mind is the ultimate driver of mastery. In this part of the book, we'll explore the role of habits in trading and why, though important, they are tools that must remain secondary to the sharpness of your thinking.

The Role of Repetition

Habits, at their core, are born from repetition. Repetition builds comfort, familiarity, and a sense of control. For traders, habits are celebrated for the consistency they create, morning routines that set the tone for the day, processes that bring order to market analysis, and routines that solidify discipline. Repetition can turn a complex task into something intuitive, reducing mental friction and making actions feel effortless.

However, repetition can also lead to complacency. Habits followed blindly can become limiting. Traders often fall into the trap of assuming that once a habit is established, the work is done. They become so attached to their routines that they stop questioning their relevance. What happens when the market shifts, but your habits don't? What happens when you've built an unshakable routine, but it no longer serves you?

Relying on habits alone can leave you vulnerable. If you become too dependent on a specific routine or strategy, you may fail to recognize when it's time to adapt. The master strategist understands that habits are a starting point, but they must be accompanied by the willingness to evolve. The ability to rethink and adjust your habits as the market evolves is what separates those who succeed from those who fall behind. Habits are valuable tools, but they must always remain open to refinement.

The Habit of Adaptation

The most powerful habit you can cultivate as a trader is the habit of adapting. In an ever-changing market, the ability to adjust and evolve is invaluable. While external habits like reviewing charts, setting risk parameters, and executing trades are essential, it's the internal habit of mental flexibility that will keep you thriving in volatile environments.

Many traders cling to methods that worked in the past, hoping the market will align with their expectations. But the market doesn't care about your expectations. It's constantly shifting, evolving, and presenting new challenges. The most dangerous assumption a trader can make is believing that what worked yesterday will always work tomorrow.

The habit of adaptation is about learning to be fluid, to adjust not only in response to losses but also in anticipation of market changes. Traders who master the habit of adaptation aren't thrown off balance by unexpected shifts, they've trained themselves to expect the unexpected. They're always ready to pivot, to adjust their strategy, and to think critically about their next move.

Adaptation isn't about abandoning structure, but about building a structure that allows for flexibility. The master strategist recognizes that habits should never be rigid. Instead, they should provide stability while maintaining the flexibility to evolve when necessary. In this way, adaptation becomes a habit in itself—a tool for staying sharp, for learning continuously, and for remaining resilient in the face of uncertainty.

Habits and Discipline

Discipline is often hailed as the cornerstone of success, and for good reason. Without discipline, even the best habits will fall apart. Discipline allows you to follow through on your strategies, remain consistent, and stay focused. It's the force that turns habits into a reliable system.

However, discipline can sometimes be mistaken for rigidity. The disciplined trader is often seen as one who follows their routine without question, sticking to their habits no matter what. But true discipline isn't about blindly following a set of rules—it's about maintaining focus while knowing when it's time to adjust. Discipline is not about mindlessly repeating the same actions, but about staying committed to the bigger picture while being open to change.

Take, for example, a trading habit that revolves around a particular set of indicators. Discipline might mean adhering to this method even in volatile market conditions. But what happens when those indicators stop providing accurate signals? What if the market environment has shifted so dramatically that your tried-and-true strategy no longer works?

This is where discipline must be paired with flexibility. The disciplined trader knows when to follow their routine, but also when to rethink their approach. They understand that the market is constantly changing, and their habits must evolve accordingly. Discipline supports habits, but it must always be balanced with adaptability. Without this balance, discipline turns into rigidity, and rigidity is the enemy of progress.

The Power of Reflection

The key takeaway is this: habits are tools, not rules. They are meant to serve you, not to bind you. The moment a habit becomes a rigid rule is the moment it loses its value. The master strategist knows that habits must be fluid, always open to refinement and change.

As you develop your trading habits, focus on flexibility. Build routines that provide structure, but don't be afraid to adjust them as needed. Success doesn't come from following the same routine day in and day out, it comes from knowing when to shift, when to adapt, and when to rethink.

Habits are powerful, but they are secondary to the mind's ability to grow. It's the mind that drives success. Habits support it, but they should never take control. The true master strategist knows that while habits may provide a framework for success, it is the mind, flexible, adaptable, and ever-evolving—that is the true key to mastery.

Part 2

Foresight : Seeing Beyond the Present Trade

Foresight is the unseen thread that runs through every successful trade, decision, and strategy. It's not just about predicting where the market will move next, but understanding the subtle interplay between your mind, the data, and the infinite possibilities of the market. To become a master strategist, foresight is your sharpest tool. It's the ability to anticipate not just the future, but the many potential futures that could unfold, and preparing yourself for any outcome.

At the heart of foresight lies the brain's extraordinary capacity for prediction. Whether you're aware of it or not, your brain is constantly predicting, matching patterns, and thinking ahead, long before you consciously decide on your next move. The difference between an average trader and a master strategist lies in the ability to harness this natural predictive power, refine it, and use it to outmaneuver the market.

Chapter 5

The Brain: A Predicting Machine

Imagine stepping into the world with no understanding of what's next, each moment would be overwhelming, chaotic, a flood of sensory information. Fortunately, your brain doesn't allow that to happen. Instead, it operates like a master strategist, tirelessly working to predict what will come next based on past experience, patterns, and learned knowledge. It's the ultimate survival mechanism, honed over millennia, making sense of the world not by reacting to it, but by predicting it.

At the heart of every decision you make, every step you take, lies the brain's remarkable ability to forecast. It's constantly calculating outcomes, comparing what's happening in the moment to what it expects to happen, and adjusting as needed. This ability to predict is not just a biological trick, it's the very essence of how we function. In trading, in life, in every endeavor, success depends on how well your brain predicts and adapts to the future.

The Inner Workings of Prediction

The brain is not a passive receiver of information; it's an active architect of perception. When you look at a familiar chart, for instance, your brain is not merely absorbing data in real time. Instead, it's rapidly scanning for patterns, comparing them with previous experiences, and attempting to forecast what will happen next. This is why, as traders, you can often sense the direction of the market before the movement occurs.

Neuroscientists call this process "predictive coding". Your brain continuously generates hypotheses about what's likely to happen in the immediate future based on past input. It's an efficient system: rather than processing each piece of data afresh, the brain works with predictions. If a prediction matches reality, all is well. If there's a mismatch, your brain updates its model of the world.

Think about the last time you were walking in a familiar environment. You didn't need to consciously focus on every step or object. Your brain filled in the gaps, predicting where each obstacle would be, guiding your actions effortlessly. It's the same mechanism at play when you anticipate market behavior in trading. Over time, your brain becomes attuned to certain signals, trends, and rhythms, creating a mental model of the market that helps guide your decisions.

But, like any system, prediction is imperfect. Mismatches between expectation and reality lead to moments of surprise or confusion. In trading, this might be a sudden price movement that catches you off guard. How you respond to these moments —whether you cling to your predictions or adjust swiftly, an make the difference between success and failure

Patterns: The Brain's Best Friend

The brain is a master at recognizing patterns. From the earliest days of human evolution, this skill has been crucial for survival. Spotting patterns in weather, in the behavior of predators, or in the movement of prey gave our gave our ancestors a distinct advantage. Today, that same pattern recognition is what traders rely on when they scan market charts or interpret data points.

When you see a familiar setup in the market, a technical indicator aligning with a price movement, your brain is drawing on stored patterns to make a prediction. It's telling you, based on past experiences, that this setup often leads to a certain outcome. This is where the brain's predictive ability shines. You can anticipate the market's next move because you've seen it before, countless times.

However, the danger lies in the brain's over-reliance on familiar patterns. Markets are dynamic, constantly shifting and evolving. What worked yesterday may not work tomorrow, and the brain's desire for consistency can sometimes lead to cognitive bias. This is why successful traders are those who blend their brain's natural pattern recognition with a willingness to rethink and adapt. The brain's predictions are invaluable, but they must be balanced with flexibility and open-mindedness.

The Role of Uncertainty

The market is uncertain. Life, for that matter, is uncertain. Yet the brain craves certainty. It's hardwired to reduce ambiguity and predict what's next. This creates a tension in trading: the market thrives on unpredictability, while your brain thrives on predictability.

So how does a brain wired for certainty cope with a world that refuses to be fully predictable? It adapts through probabilities. Rather than offering absolute outcomes, the brain provides you with predictions framed in likelihoods. When you place a trade, your brain isn't saying, "This will happen." It's saying, "Based on what I know, this is the most probable outcome." The ability to accept and work within this probabilistic framework is key to thriving in uncertain environments like the financial markets.

However, many traders struggle with this. When a trade doesn't go their way, they may feel as if the market betrayed them or that they failed. In reality, the brain was simply making the best prediction it could with the available information. It wasn't a guarantee, just an educated guess. The best traders embrace this uncertainty. They understand that not every prediction will be right, but every prediction provides valuable data to refine future forecasts.

Prediction and Emotion

Prediction doesn't just happen at the intellectual level; it's deeply intertwined with emotion. When your brain predicts that something good is about to happen, like a successful trade—you experience positive emotions. When it predicts failure or danger, you feel anxiety, fear, or frustration. These emotional responses can be incredibly powerful motivators or demotivators, influencing your decision-making in subtle and not-so-subtle ways.

In trading, emotional management is often the difference between winning and losing. A trader whose predictions consistently mismatch reality may feel discouraged, leading to rash decisions. On the flip side, a trader whose predictions align with the market might feel overconfident, leading to careless risk-taking.

Understanding that your emotions are directly tied to your brain's predictions can help you manage them more effectively. When a trade goes against you, instead of reactingemotionally, you can remind yourself that it's just a mismatch between prediction and outcome. The brain isn't perfect, and every mistake is a learning opportunity. With this mindset, you can approach trading with a sense of calm and control, even when your predictions fail.

The Power of Learning

The brain's predictive abilities are not fixed, they evolve. Every experience, every success, every failure reshapes the brain's model of the world. In trading, this is especially important. The more you learn from your trades, the more accurate your predictions become.

This is why reflection is a critical part of trading. After each trade, whether it was successful or not, taking the time to analyze what happened strengthens your brain's future predictions. What signals did you miss? What patterns emerged? What could you have done differently? Each of these reflections feeds into the brain's predictive machinery, sharpening it for future trades.

But it's not just about learning from mistakes. Celebrating successes and understanding why they worked is equally important. When your brain accurately predicts an outcome, it strengthens the neural pathways associated with that prediction, making it easier to replicate in the future. This is why disciplined traders, who consistently review and reflect on their performance, tend to improve over time, they are actively training their brains to predict more effectively.Act as if you are the gravity write feature image prompt. A book bring written. Make it realistic and 3D

The Balance Between Prediction and adaption

While the brain's ability to predict is remarkable, there's a fine line between relying on those predictions and becoming rigid in your thinking. The market, like life, is ever-changing, and no prediction is guaranteed to be right. That's why the best traders are those who balance their brain's predictions with a willingness to adapt.

In trading, this means being open to the idea that your predictions will sometimes be wrong, and that's okay. It's about knowing when to trust your brain's forecast and when to step back, reassess, and adjust your approach. Adaptability is the key to longevity in a market that can shift direction in an instant.

Your brain is a powerful predicting machine, but it's also a flexible one. The more you engage with uncertainty, reflect on your experiences, and remain open to change, the more refined your brain's predictions become. In the world of trading, this balance between prediction and adaptation is the hallmark of a true master.

Embracing the Predictive Mind

To succeed in trading, or any endeavor, for that matter, you must recognize the incredible predictive power of your brain. It is constantly working, behind the scenes, to help you navigate the complexities of life and the market. By understanding how your brain predicts, how it learns from mismatches, and how it manages uncertainty, you can become more in tune with your decision-making process.

The brain's predictions are not about crystal-clear certainty—they are about probabilities, about making the best-educated guess based on past patterns. As a trader, your job is to refine those predictions through learning, reflection, and adaptation.

In the end, the brain is not just a predicting machine, it's a learning machine, constantly evolving, constantly adjusting, and constantly preparing you for whatever comes next. And in a world as unpredictable as the market, that is the greatest tool you can have.

Chapter 6

Thinking in Scenarios : Crafting Future Possibilities

Imagine being a chess player not focused on just the next move but the entire board, a strategist who sees beyond the obvious, preparing for every possible shift in the game. This is the essence of scenario thinking. It's the art of holding multiple futures in your mind at once, crafting responses for each, and navigating uncertainty with calm precision. For a master strategist, thinking in scenarios is not about guessing what "will" happen, but about being ready for "anything" that might happen. The question is never, "What do I think will happen?" but rather, "What are all the ways this could play out, and how will I respond?"

The Power of Expanding Your Vision

When we think in straight lines, expecting things to unfold exactly as we predict, we blind ourselves to the richness of possibilities. Scenario thinking breaks that pattern. It requires you to take off the blinders and expand your vision to embrace uncertainty, recognizing that reality is rarely a single path but a web of interconnected possibilities.

For a trader, this means looking beyond the immediate price movements or economic news and understanding that markets shift, sometimes suddenly and without warning. The savvy strategist knows that planning for a single outcome is akin to walking on thin ice. To truly thrive, you need to prepare for the moments when the ground shifts beneath you.

But this isn't about being paralyzed by possibilities. On the contrary, it's about empowering yourself with a wider perspective. You don't need to predict the exact course of future events. You only need to map out several plausible futures and prepare yourself for any one of them, ready to adapt at a moment's notice.

Mapping the Terrain of Possibilities

To think in scenarios is to become a mental cartographer, sketching out the terrain of possibilities before you. Here's how you begin:

1. Define the Decision: You start by asking, "What is the challenge or decision I'm facing?" The clearer you are about the decision at hand, the easier it becomes to construct the scenarios around it. Whether you're entering a trade, launching a new product, or rethinking a business strategy, clarity here is vital.

2. Identify the Drivers: Next, you pinpoint the forces that could shape your future. What are the major variables at play? For a trader, this might include market sentiment, economic indicators, or geopolitical events. In business, it could be emerging technologies, competitive moves, or regulatory changes. These variables become the levers that create your scenarios.

3. Craft the Scenarios: Now comes the creative part, imagine different futures. Picture a world where the market surges, and then one where it crashes. Picture a future where your competitors innovate faster than you, or where they falter. Sketch out best-case, worst-case, and middle-ground scenarios. Each scenario tells a different story about the future, and your job is to inhabit each one fully, thinking through its implications.

Turning Uncertainty Into Opportunity

One of the greatest misconceptions is that thinking in scenarios is about fear, about being ready for everything that could go wrong. But it's not just about preparing for the worst; it's about being primed for opportunities that others might miss.

When you approach a situation with multiple scenarios in mind, you open yourself up to unexpected possibilities. You might spot an opportunity in the middle of chaos or a chance to pivot when conditions change. This kind of foresight is what allows the master strategist to capitalize when others are stuck in reaction mode, clinging to their singular expectations.

The Flexibility of a Shapeshifter

The ability to think in scenarios requires a mental flexibility that many people don't cultivate. The brain loves certainty, it craves simplicity, a clear path forward. But the strategist must train their mind to love ambiguity, to dance in the space between possibilities.

Thinking in scenarios means becoming comfortable with not knowing. It's about shifting between different futures in your mind, letting go of rigid plans and becoming adaptable. You are not a tree rooted in place, but a shapeshifter who can move with the changing winds.

When the market crashes, the thinker in scenarios isn't frozen with panic. They've already considered this. They've seen this future in their mind and are ready to execute their next move.

When competitors surprise you, you don't falter. You've built in contingency plans and prepared for pivots.

Mastering the Art of the "What If"

Thinking in scenarios is built on one powerful question: What if?

"What if the market drops 10% tomorrow?"
"What if a new technology renders your product obsolete?"
"What if a new regulation wipes out your competitive edge?"

But it's not enough to ask the question, you need to follow it through. The true power comes in your ability to build strategies for each "what if" scenario. This isn't about hoping for one outcome over another; it's about welcoming every possibility and being agile enough to adapt, no matter what happens.

Resilience in the Face of the Unknown

The world rewards those who can thrive in uncertainty. The strategist who thinks in scenarios is never caught off guard because they don't cling to one narrative about how the future will unfold. They've already prepared for the unexpected, so when the unexpected arrives, they meet it with calm confidence.

There's immense power in this mental resilience. It means that setbacks don't derail you; they simply trigger a shift in your strategy. You have anticipated challenges, and you have already prepared for how to respond. When others are reeling from the shock of an unanticipated change, you are already executing the next phase of your plan.

The Balance of Creativity and Logic

To be a master strategist is to be a thinker in scenarios, a mind always turning, always imagining multiple outcomes, always ready. This mindset doesn't just help you survive; it ensures you stay ahead of the game, no matter how the landscape shifts.

Thinking in scenarios isn't just about preparation, it's about empowering yourself with foresight, adaptability, and resilience. With this mindset, you don't just respond to change; you anticipate it, welcome it, and use it to your advantage.

Chapter 7

Mastery in Planning: The Blueprint for Trading Success

Planning is the cornerstone of success in trading, as well as in any venture that requires strategic thinking. But planning is not about having a rigid roadmap that locks you into a single path. Instead, it's about developing a flexible framework that allows you to navigate uncertainty, anticipate changes, and pivot when the market or environment demands it. A master strategist doesn't plan for certainty, they plan for the unpredictable, turning chaos into opportunity.

For traders, planning is often seen as a tool to create order in the wild world of the markets. However, the markets are alive —constantly shifting and evolving. Success comes not from predicting the future perfectly, but from having a plan that can adapt as that future unfolds. In trading, just like in life, the more adaptable your plan, the more resilient you will be when the unexpected happens.

The Paradox of Planning: Stability Through Adaptability

In trading, a paradox emerges: the best plans provide both stability and adaptability. At first glance, these two might seem at odds. Stability suggests consistency, a firm foundation from which to execute your trades. Adaptability, on the other hand, requires flexibility, an ability to shift course when the conditions change. Yet, the master strategist knows that true planning must incorporate both.

A good trading plan creates a structured process, an outline that governs how you enter and exit trades, manage risk, and protect your capital. This structure is crucial because it gives you a roadmap to follow, reducing impulsive decisions driven by emotion or market noise. Without a plan, traders often fall into the trap of chasing the market, reacting to every price movement without a clear sense of purpose.

But, and this is where most traders fall short, a plan that is too rigid can become a trap. The market is constantly evolving, and a strategy that works in one environment might fail in another. Traders who stick doggedly to a plan without adjusting for new information or changing market conditions often find themselves on the wrong side of trades. Planning in trading must be dynamic, not static. You create a plan to guide your actions, but you must also know when to adapt.

Think about how an experienced sailor navigates the sea. They might chart a course before setting sail, but they also know that the wind, currents, and weather are unpredictable. The best sailors are those who can adjust their sails and alter their course when necessary while still keeping the destination in mind. Similarly, in trading, you need a plan that offers direction but remains flexible enough to adapt to the winds of change that blow through the markets.

For example, consider a trader who uses a trend-following strategy. Their plan might be to enter trades when an asset breaks above a moving average and to exit when the trend reverses. This plan works well in trending markets. However, when the market becomes choppy or range-bound, this strategy might lead to multiple false signals, resulting in losses. A rigid trader might continue executing the plan blindly, despite the changing conditions, while a master strategist recognizes the need to adapt the plan or sit out during uncertain times.

From Blueprint to Execution: The Trader's Dilemma

One of the greatest challenges traders face is the leap from planning to execution. It's easy to draw up the perfect trading plan, one that outlines entry and exit points, risk management rules, and capital allocation strategies. But the market is rarely as cooperative as your plan suggests. Once you move from the planning phase to the execution phase, you'll encounter the friction of reality volatility, unforeseen news events, emotional reactions, and the unpredictable behavior of other traders.

In trading, the market is the ultimate test of any plan. No matter how thorough your analysis or how well-crafted your strategy, the market will present situations you didn't anticipate. This is where execution becomes an art form, where improvisation, mental flexibility, and discipline come into play.

The market isn't static. It's a living, breathing organism influenced by countless factors, macro events, investor sentiment, technological advancements, and geopolitical dynamics. No matter how well you plan, there will always be an element of the unknown. The master trader acknowledges this reality and prepares for it. They know that successful execution requires the ability to think on their feet, adjust their approach, and make decisions based on what the market is telling them in real time, not just what they planned for in advance.

In fact, some of the greatest traders in history, people like George Soros, Paul Tudor Jones, and Jesse Livermore built their legacies not by sticking rigidly to their plans, but by mastering the ability to adapt and improvise. Soros, for example, was known for abandoning his own carefully laid-out strategies when he sensed a shift in market conditions. Livermore famously rode market crashes by recognizing the moment when the market had changed, despite his original plans.

Improvisation in trading doesn't mean abandoning your plan at the first sign of trouble. It means having the wisdom to know when a plan is no longer serving you and the courage to adjust it. The trader who can improvise while staying true to their overarching goals will always outperform the one who rigidly sticks to a fixed path, even as the ground shifts beneath them.

This is where the importance of scenario thinking comes into play. A trader who can anticipate multiple outcomes is better equipped to adjust their plan when necessary. They don't just have a single blueprint; they have a range of possibilities and can move fluidly between them based on the unfolding situation. By incorporating scenario thinking into their planning process, they build the mental agility needed to execute effectively in any market condition.

Planning for the Unknown: Building Resilience in Trading

One of the most common mistakes traders make is planning as though they can eliminate uncertainty. The reality is that uncertainty is an inherent part of the markets. You will never have perfect information, and you will never be able to predict every market movement. However, planning for the unknown is not only possible but essential.

How do you plan for something you can't predict? The key lies in building resilience. Resilient traders understand that uncertainty is not an obstacle to be feared, but an opportunity to be embraced. They don't waste energy trying to eliminate uncertainty. Instead, they focus on building a trading system that can thrive in uncertain conditions.

This is where the concept of scenario planning becomes a powerful tool. Instead of crafting a single plan based on a specific prediction about the market, you create a range of potential scenarios. You ask yourself: What if the market rises? What if it falls? What if it stays flat? What if a major geopolitical event occurs? What if central banks change their policies? By considering multiple scenarios, you are mentally prepared for a wider range of outcomes.

In scenario thinking, each outcome is seen as a potential path to success. You prepare for volatility, but you don't fear it. When a scenario materializes, you have a plan ready to execute. This doesn't mean you can predict the future with perfect accuracy, but it does mean that you are ready to act, regardless of what happens.

For example, imagine you're a trader focused on a particular stock. You might plan for three scenarios: one where the stock price increases, one where it decreases, and one where it trades sideways. For each scenario, you outline the trades you'll take, the risks you'll manage, and the signals you'll watch for. Then, as the market unfolds, you adjust your strategy according to the scenario that's playing out in real time.

This approach creates resilience. Instead of panicking when the market doesn't behave as you expected, you're able to pivot quickly and act decisively. Planning for the unknown doesn't mean predicting the future, it means preparing yourself mentally, emotionally, and strategically to succeed no matter what the future holds.

The Art of Strategic Planning in Trading

At its core, planning in trading is about creating a framework that allows you to navigate uncertainty with confidence. It's not about predicting the market with perfect accuracy or creating a rigid strategy that never changes. Instead, it's about crafting a plan that provides structure and direction while remaining flexible enough to adapt as new information becomes available.

Mastery in planning comes from understanding that the best plans are those that evolve. The market is unpredictable, but by planning for multiple scenarios and building resilience into your strategy, you can thrive in the face of uncertainty.

Part 3

The Strategist's Blueprint: Mastering the Foundation of Insights

Every master strategist knows that a blueprint is more than just a plan, it's a vision brought to life through meticulous design, thoughtful consideration, and a deep understanding of what has come before. In the same way an architect uses the laws of physics and the wisdom of past structures to create something enduring, the trader relies on history to guide their next move and build their strategy around a single asset.

But this blueprint is not rigid; it's dynamic, evolving with each new insight. A true strategist doesn't just rely on instinct or the heat of the moment. They learn from past patterns, understanding the subtle currents of market history, and distill their focus into mastering one key asset. With every scenario, every shift, they recalibrate, adjusting their framework to suit the moment. This is the essence of the strategist's blueprint: a map drawn from past experiences but flexible enough to conquer the unknown futures ahead.

Chapter 8

History: The key

Imagine walking through a maze with no idea of the twists and turns ahead. Each path feels like a gamble, and every wrong turn costs time and energy. Now, picture being handed a detailed map, showing you every dead end and shortcut. Suddenly, the maze isn't as daunting, and your journey becomes far more strategic.

In trading, history is that map. It offers insights not just into successes, but also the mistakes others have made. Markets, despite their chaos, move in cycles—, patterns that, when studied, help traders navigate with greater precision. These cycles reveal trends and behaviors that repeat over time, allowing traders to anticipate future moves.

Trading without understanding market history is like navigating blind. You may find success occasionally, but it will be based on luck, not strategy. Those who embrace history gain a critical advantage, learning from the past to better understand the present and plan for the future. This chapter explores why understanding market history is essential to becoming a master strategist.

The Market's Memory: Understanding Patterns and Cycles

To the untrained eye, the stock market seems like an unpredictable force, driven by news, emotion, and random fluctuations. But beneath the surface lies a rhythm, a heartbeat of sorts, that has repeated itself throughout history. This rhythm can be identified in cycles: boom and bust, bull and bear, expansion and contraction. These cycles are driven by the collective psychology of market participants, which tends to repeat itself in response to similar stimuli.

For example, consider the financial bubbles that have marked history. The Dutch tulip mania in the 17th century, the South Sea Bubble, the Roaring Twenties stock market bubble, the Dot-com boom, and the housing market bubble all share a common theme. In each case, market participants became overly optimistic, driving prices to unsustainable levels. Greed took over, leading to irrational exuberance, followed by a sharp and painful collapse when reality caught up.

The lesson here is simple: while the market may seem unpredictable in the short term, long-term cycles driven by human emotion, fear and greed tend to repeat. Traders who study these historical bubbles can recognize when the market is behaving irrationally and prepare accordingly. Instead of getting swept up in the hype, they remain grounded, knowing that history has shown them what comes next.

Take the Dow Theory, for instance, which is rooted in the idea that market movements are not random but occur in discernible phases. According to the theory, a market cycle consists of three phases: accumulation, participation, and distribution. Understanding where the market currently resides in this cycle helps traders determine whether they should be entering or exiting positions. Traders who study history don't just react to current market conditions, they anticipate what's likely to come next.

This historical perspective gives traders an invaluable edge. When the market starts behaving irrationally, they don't panic or get caught up in the frenzy. Instead, they lean on the patterns and cycles they've studied, recognizing that while the future may be uncertain, it is rarely completely unpredictable.

Learning from Legends: Strategies Rooted in History

Trading strategies are not invented in a vacuum. The greatest traders in history didn't stumble upon success by chance. Instead, they studied the markets meticulously, learned from their predecessors, and developed strategies that stood the test of time. Their methods, rooted in history, provide valuable lessons for today's traders, especially those willing to learn from both their successes and failures.

Warren Buffett is a prime example of a trader who built his success on the lessons of the past. Buffett is a disciple of Benjamin Graham, who is considered the father of value investing. Graham's teachings, which emphasized buying stocks at prices below their intrinsic value, were developed during the Great Depression, a time when the stock market was deeply undervalued, and panic dominated investor behavior.

Graham's philosophy was simple: when fear drives prices below their true worth, investors have an opportunity to buy stocks at a discount. This strategy requires patience, discipline, and, most importantly, a historical understanding of market overreactions. Buffett took Graham's teachings and applied them to his own strategy, becoming one of the richest and most successful investors in history. His approach, rooted in a historical understanding of market psychology, emphasizes long-term investing and avoiding the short-term noise that often leads traders astray.

On the other end of the spectrum, we have traders like George Soros, whose success came not from holding positions long-term but from understanding how markets behave in times of crisis. Soros famously bet against the British pound in 1992, making over a billion dollars in a single day. His strategy was based on his deep understanding of historical economic conditions and the behavior of central banks during times of financial stress.

Soros didn't just guess that the pound would collapse—he studied the historical precedents of currency interventions, recognized the unsustainable nature of the British government's position, and acted accordingly. His ability to connect historical patterns with current events allowed him to capitalize on one of the greatest trades of all time.

The takeaway here is clear: history doesn't just provide lessons in what "not" to do; it also offers a roadmap to success. By studying the strategies of past masters, traders can refine their own approaches, avoiding the pitfalls that have trapped others while capitalizing on opportunities that others might miss. Whether you're a long-term investor like Buffett or a short-term speculator like Soros, history provides the blueprint for success.

Pitfalls and Progress: The Evolution of Strategy

While history is an invaluable tool for traders, it's also important to recognize that the market evolves. Strategies that worked in the past may not always work in the future, and traders must adapt their approaches to changing conditions. History provides the foundation, but the ability to evolve is what separates good traders from great ones.

Consider the rise of algorithmic trading. In the early days of the market, traders relied on paper charts, human intuition, and basic technical analysis to make their decisions. Today, however, sophisticated algorithms can analyze vast amounts of data in seconds, executing trades at lightning speed. Traders who fail to adapt to these technological advancements risk being left behind.

But even as the market evolves, the core principles remain the same. Human psychology, fear, greed, hope, and panic, continues to drive market behavior, just as it did centuries ago. The key is to blend historical knowledge with modern innovation. Traders who study the past and embrace the tools of the future are the ones who will thrive in today's rapidly changing market.

For instance, during the 2008 financial crisis, many traders who ignored the warning signs of historical bubbles lost everything. But those who had studied the housing bubble of the 1920s, the tech bubble of the 1990s, and the many other speculative frenzies throughout history recognized the same patterns of irrational exuberance. They knew that when prices become detached from reality, a crash is imminent.

However, it's important to remember that while history provides valuable lessons, it is not a crystal ball. The market will always have an element of unpredictability. The goal is not to predict every move perfectly but to increase your odds of success by understanding the broader context. History teaches us to prepare for the unexpected, to anticipate risks, and to act decisively when opportunity arises.

The greatest traders are not those who simply memorize historical facts. They are the ones who understand the "why" behind those facts, who study not just the outcomes but the underlying causes. They use this knowledge to adapt their strategies in real-time, always ready to adjust course when the market shifts.

Embracing History as a Strategic Tool

In trading, history is more than just a record of what happened. It's a guidebook, a teacher, and a warning. Traders who ignore history do so at their own peril, blindly navigating the market without a compass. But those who embrace the lessons of the past, who study the cycles, learn from the masters, and recognize the ever-present patterns in human behavior, hold a distinct advantage.

History provides the foundation for every successful strategy. It teaches us about the market's cycles, the behavior of investors, and the strategies that have stood the test of time. But it also teaches us the importance of adaptability. The market is constantly evolving, and traders must evolve with it, blending historical knowledge with modern innovation.

To become a master strategist, you must view history not as a static record but as a living, breathing tool that informs every decision you make. By studying the past, you can navigate the present with greater clarity and prepare for the future with confidence. In the end, history is the key to unlocking the full potential of your trading strategy.

Chapter 9

Mastering One Asset: The Power of Focus

Focusing on a single asset in trading is like studying the intricacies of one instrument in a symphony. When you dedicate yourself to understanding that asset inside and out, you develop an instinctual ability to anticipate its movements, its tendencies, and its reactions. This level of attention separates the casual trader from the master strategist. While many emphasize the need for diversification, spreading their attention across numerous markets, there is a strong case for focusing on one asset. Deep focus allows you to truly master the rhythm and patterns that may otherwise be missed in the noise of multiple markets.

For a trader who focuses on Bitcoin, the asset becomes more than just a line on a chart or a ticker to watch. It becomes a living, breathing entity with its own unique characteristics. You notice how it behaves in different market environments, how it reacts to certain kinds of news, and how its volatility spikes at certain times of day. This intimate understanding allows you to make better-informed decisions, anticipate market moves, and develop a trading strategy that is far more nuanced and sophisticated than if you were juggling multiple assets at once.

Seeing the unseen:
The power of focused attention

In trading, attention is everything. The more focused your attention, the more details you observe that others might miss. Think of it like observing a piece of art. From a distance, you might only see the broad strokes, the general colors, and the overall composition. But if you step closer, paying careful attention to every brushstroke, every detail, you begin to see the hidden elements that give the painting depth. The same is true in trading, when you zoom in on a single asset, you begin to see its intricacies that other traders, distracted by multiple markets, might overlook.

For example, let's consider Bitcoin. Most traders understand that Bitcoin can be highly volatile and is sensitive to macroeconomic factors like inflation, regulation, or institutional adoption. But when you dedicate yourself to studying Bitcoin over time, you start to notice things others miss, such as how Bitcoin tends to behave in certain seasons, how market sentiment changes after key news events, or how certain patterns repeat themselves based on liquidity flows from large holders known as "whales." You also begin to see how Bitcoin correlates with other assets like tech stocks or gold at different times.

More importantly, you gain a feel for the asset's psychology. Unlike stocks, where earnings reports and company fundamentals are critical drivers, Bitcoin is driven by a mix of technological innovation, speculative interest, regulatory concerns, and cultural shifts in how people view digital assets.

As you focus on Bitcoin, you develop an intuition for when speculative bubbles are forming, when the asset is being driven by fear, and when a potential buying or selling opportunity may present itself based on historical patterns.

This level of insight is difficult to achieve when you're juggling multiple assets. Traders who divide their attention across several markets often miss these small, telling signs that an asset is about to shift. When you focus your attention on one asset, you begin to see the market in high resolution, noticing the subtle changes that signal an opportunity or a potential risk.

Reacting with Precision: Mastering Timing and Execution

The ability to react with precision is one of the most powerful benefits of focusing on a single asset. Each asset in the financial markets reacts differently to macroeconomic events, news, and technical conditions. While some assets may spike in volatility during certain times of day or after specific events, others may move more predictably. The key to trading successfully is knowing "how" and "when" to react, and that requires a deep understanding of the asset's behavior.

For instance, Bitcoin, compared to other traditional assets, has its own unique cycles driven by factors such as halving events, regulatory developments, and even social media trends. As a Bitcoin trader who devotes their attention to mastering this one asset, you start to understand its daily, weekly, and yearly cycles. You know that volatility tends to spike during certain times of the day, particularly when both U.S. and Asian markets overlap. You also know how the asset responds to big announcements, like new regulations or technological upgrades in the blockchain space.

Having such specific knowledge allows you to react faster and more accurately than traders who are less familiar with the asset. Timing is everything in the markets, executing a trade even a few seconds too early or too late can be the difference between a profitable trade and a loss. When you focus on one asset, you develop a finely tuned sense of timing. You're not just reacting to broad market moves but anticipating them based on your intimate knowledge of the asset.

For example, if you've studied Bitcoin's reaction to Federal Reserve announcements or the release of economic data, you know how it typically moves following these events. More importantly, you can plan your trades with greater precision, positioning yourself before the move happens, not after. This level of anticipation is only possible when you focus deeply on a single asset.

Mastery Through Deep Knowledge: Becoming a Specialist

There's an old saying that goes, "Jack of all trades, master of none." While it's tempting to spread yourself across many assets in the hopes of catching more opportunities, there's an undeniable power in becoming a specialist. When you dedicate your attention to mastering one asset, you build a deep well of knowledge that most traders simply don't have. You move from being a generalist who knows a little about everything to being a master who knows everything about one thing.

In the context of Bitcoin, becoming a specialist means going beyond price charts and technical indicators. It means understanding Bitcoin's underlying technology, its historical price action, and its market structure. You need to know about the asset's supply dynamics—like Bitcoin's fixed supply cap of 21 million coins and how halving events impact its inflation rate. You must also grasp the cultural and ideological forces that drive adoption, as Bitcoin's rise is often linked to a larger societal shift toward decentralization and distrust in traditional financial systems.

By mastering one asset, you also understand its risks and opportunities on a much deeper level. For instance, a Bitcoin specialist knows that, while the asset can experience massive rallies, it's also prone to sharp corrections, often driven by sentiment rather than fundamentals. You learn to recognize when the market is overheated, when it's driven by hype, and when a more cautious approach is warranted.

As a Bitcoin specialist, you can also predict how different market participants will behave in certain conditions. You'll know that retail traders tend to panic during sharp corrections, while institutional traders may see such dips as buying opportunities. You'll also understand the role of large holders—whales, and how their buying or selling can drive significant market moves. This depth of understanding helps you navigate the market with greater confidence, making more informed decisions based on your extensive knowledge.

The Path to Mastery

Mastering one asset is not just about simplifying your trading process, it's about deepening your understanding, refining your strategies, and gaining a competitive edge in a crowded market. While many traders chase the allure of diversification, spreading their attention across multiple markets, the true power lies in focus. By dedicating yourself to one asset, you gain a level of mastery that few traders achieve. You begin to see the market in high definition, noticing patterns, reactions, and behaviors that others miss.

For Bitcoin traders, this deep focus allows you to anticipate moves, react with precision, and develop a strategy rooted in intimate knowledge of the asset's unique characteristics. You move beyond surface-level analysis, diving deep into the psychology, market structure, and technological fundamentals that drive Bitcoin's price. Over time, this focus on one asset transforms you from a reactive trader into a proactive strategist, someone who doesn't just follow the market, but anticipates its moves with confidence and clarity.

In the end, the path to mastery is not about knowing everything, it's about knowing one thing better than anyone else. For the master strategist, focus is the key to unlocking deeper insights, sharper execution, and long-term success in the market. By narrowing your focus to one asset, you create the foundation for a more disciplined, informed, and profitable trading approach.

Chapter 10

The Strategy: Building the Blueprint

Building a trading strategy is like solving a puzzle, but the pieces come from both the "past" and the" present". In the previous chapters, we explored two vital ideas: how history reveals market patterns, and the value of mastering "one asset". These concepts are the foundation of any successful strategy.

In "Chapter 6" , we learned that "history is key" , providing insight into recurring market cycles and helping us avoid past mistakes. In "Chapter 7" , we focused on the importance of specializing in "one asset" , like Bitcoin, to truly understand its behavior.

Now, we bring these lessons together to craft a strategy. A master strategist doesn't just react to the market but creates a proactive, adaptable plan, grounded in historical foresight and a deep understanding of a specific asset.

Laying the Foundation: Bringing History into Focus

The foundation of any trading strategy lies in how well you've understood and internalized history. History isn't just a vague recollection of past price action, it's the key to understanding how markets "think" and react under different conditions. In the world of Bitcoin, this is even more crucial. Bitcoin's price has followed dramatic cycles: the rise and fall after halving events, the euphoric highs driven by retail investors, and the sharp corrections that follow.

By studying these historical cycles, you can predict potential turning points. History reveals how Bitcoin reacts to certain stimuli, be it technological advancements, regulatory announcements, or macroeconomic conditions. For example, Bitcoin's repeated price surges following its halving events are not coincidences, they are part of a larger market structure driven by supply shocks. By integrating this knowledge into your strategy, you can position yourself ahead of major moves.

When constructing your strategy, you must begin by understanding how historical patterns influence future trends. Look back at Bitcoin's previous bull and bear markets, study the psychological behaviors of investors during key moments, and note how external events such as economic crises or government regulations have affected its price. By grounding your strategy in history, you build a foundation that prepares you to navigate the market with foresight rather than fear.

Mastering One Asset: Focusing on Bitcoin

In the last chapter, we discussed the power of mastering a single asset. When you focus on one asset like Bitcoin, you begin to see subtle shifts that others might overlook. You develop a sense for its rhythms, understanding when it's likely to enter a period of accumulation or distribution, when volatility is about to spike, and how news events tend to impact its price.

A trader who knows Bitcoin inside and out will be better equipped to anticipate its behavior than one who spreads their attention across multiple markets. It's the same principle as knowing every twist and turn of a race track, you learn to navigate it more efficiently than someone unfamiliar with the course. By dedicating yourself to one asset, you sharpen your edge.

For example, while a new trader might panic during a sharp correction, a seasoned Bitcoin trader understands that volatility is part of its DNA. They've seen it before. They recognize the signs of a price pullback that often precedes a larger rally, or how periods of low volatility often signal a coming breakout. Focusing on one asset gives you this sixth sense, a kind of intuition that comes not from guessing, but from intimate experience.

Your strategy should be built around the idiosyncrasies of Bitcoin: its frequent price swings, its cyclical nature, and the psychological patterns of the market participants who trade it.

While the broader cryptocurrency market is filled with potential, focusing on Bitcoin gives you a depth of understanding that translates into more precise decision-making. Once you master one asset, you can then expand to others, but your first strategy should always be built with a singular focus.

Execution: Synthesizing History and Focus into a Strategy

Now that you've grounded yourself in the past and honed your focus on one asset, it's time to build the strategy. Execution is where the theory meets practice, where you put your understanding of history and your specialized focus into action.

A successful strategy will combine the patterns you've learned from history with the deep knowledge you've gained by focusing on Bitcoin. Start by outlining your key rules:

1. Historical Context: Look at Bitcoin's past performance and identify key moments, such as halving cycles or regulatory shifts, that tend to cause significant price movements. This will form the basis of your market entry and exit points.

2. Specific Setup: Craft entry and exit points based on Bitcoin's historical behavior. Perhaps your strategy involves buying during accumulation phases and selling during euphoric highs. Or maybe it focuses on identifying low-volatility periods before a breakout.

3. Risk Management: No strategy is complete without risk management. Study past market crashes and corrections to understand how much Bitcoin can drop during a bear market. This will help you set stop losses and position sizes.

4 . Adaptability: Just as we learned from history, the market is never static. Your strategy must be flexible, allowing you to adapt to new information or shifts in market sentiment. If a major geopolitical event causes Bitcoin to behave differently than it has in the past, your strategy needs to evolve.

The key to successful execution is discipline. The best strategy in the world will fail if it's not followed consistently. Many traders abandon their strategy after a few losing trades, but history has shown that consistency is what leads to long-term success. Stick to the blueprint you've crafted, refining it only when necessary, and you'll find that the more you trust your process, the more it will reward you.

History, Focus, and Strategy: The Trader's Triad

By connecting the dots between history, asset focus, and strategic execution, you are setting yourself up for long-term success. History provides you with the blueprint, showing where past traders have faltered and succeeded. Focusing on one asset, like Bitcoin, sharpens your edge and gives you the insight needed to anticipate its moves. And, finally, executing your strategy with discipline and adaptability ensures that you are prepared to navigate the unpredictable twists and turns of the market.

This triad, "history, focus, and strategy", is the foundation of becoming a master strategist. It's not about predicting the future with certainty; it's about preparing for it with precision. When you combine these elements, you build a trading system that is both robust and adaptable, capable of withstanding the challenges that come with trading in the dynamic world of cryptocurrency.

Part 4

The Training Grounds: Where Mastery is Forged

Imagine stepping onto a battlefield without having trained, every move uncertain, every decision filled with doubt. In trading, the markets are your battleground, and the only way to emerge victorious is through rigorous preparation. The training grounds, however, are not just about learning strategies or memorizing technical patterns, they are about honing your instincts, testing your limits, and sharpening your edge. It's in the training that you develop the discipline, foresight, and adaptability needed to thrive amidst uncertainty. This is where you transform from a participant into a strategist, from a learner into a master.

Chapter 11

The Four Stages of Development: From Novice to Mastery in Trading

Becoming a master strategist in trading is not something that happens overnight. It is a journey of continuous growth, one that passes through distinct stages of development. Each stage serves a critical function in shaping a trader's mindset, skillset, and ultimately, their success in the market. These stages, much like levels in any discipline, mark the progression from uncertainty and inexperience to clarity and mastery.

In trading, the path toward excellence involves four key stages: Unconscious Incompetence, Conscious Incompetence, Conscious Competence, and Unconscious Competence. Understanding these stages not only allows traders to evaluate where they currently stand in their journey but also helps them recognize the areas that require focus and improvement. The following section explores these stages in depth, offering insights into how traders can move from being unaware of their weaknesses to mastering their craft.

Unconscious Incompetence: The Illusion of Knowledge

first stage of development in trading is known as "Unconscious Incompetence." This is the phase where the trader is unaware of how much they don't know. In this early stage, the beginner is often filled with excitement and optimism, believing that trading is far simpler than it truly is. They are drawn to the allure of quick profits, and the complexities of trading appear distant, if not invisible. This false sense of confidence can be intoxicating, making this one of the most dangerous stages in a trader's journey.

At this point, traders may believe they have a basic grasp of the markets, especially if they experience initial success. A few early wins, often the result of luck rather than skill, can reinforce the illusion that they are on the right track. With no real understanding of market behavior, they may take on unnecessary risks, jump into trades without proper analysis, and rely on impulse or tips from others to guide their decisions. In their mind, they are ready to take on the market, but in reality, they are flying blind.

Overconfidence and the Trap of Beginner's Luck

In the Unconscious Incompetence phase, traders are particularly susceptible to overconfidence. Because they don't yet recognize the complexities of trading, they mistakenly believe that their early wins are a result of skill rather than

Sheer luck. This can lead them to take larger positions or make more trades than they should, often without any real strategy or understanding of risk management.

Overconfidence at this stage can be a major pitfall. The beginner might believe that they have "figured it out" after a few profitable trades, only to be blindsided when the market turns against them. They might hold onto losing trades for too long, believing that the market will turn in their favor, or they might chase after quick profits without considering the potential downsides. This phase is marked by impulsive decisions and a lack of structure, which often leads to a string of losses.

What's dangerous about this stage is that the trader doesn't yet realize they are in over their head. They are still under the illusion that trading is straightforward, unaware that the market's movements are far more complex than they initially thought.

The Wake-Up Call

For most traders, moving out of the Unconscious Incompetence stage requires a humbling experience. Usually, this comes in the form of significant losses. It is only after they've lost money that they begin to realize that trading is not as easy as they first believed. This moment of reckoning is often the catalyst for deeper reflection and learning.

The trader begins to confront the reality of their ignorance. They recognize that there is much more to trading than simply buying and selling at the right time. It's not about luck or following the latest tips; it's about developing a solid understanding of market dynamics, creating a strategy, and maintaining the discipline to stick to that strategy. In this phase, the trader starts to appreciate the need for education, analysis, and emotional control.

Realizing one's own ignorance is a critical step toward growth. It's the moment when the trader begins to let go of the ego and accept that there is a lot to learn. It's not an easy realization, many traders will struggle with this acknowledgment, as it often involves facing the harsh truth that they are not yet equipped to succeed. But this realization is essential for progress.

The Transition to Conscious Incompetence

The path out of Unconscious Incompetence is one of humility. It's about recognizing that trading is a skill that requires practice, education, and patience. This stage can be frustrating, as the trader becomes aware of just how much they don't know, but it's also empowering because they have taken the first step toward becoming a more informed and disciplined trader.

At this stage, the trader must begin to study the market more seriously. They will likely seek out books, courses, or mentors to help them understand the deeper aspects of trading. The recognition of their incompetence is not a failure; it's the beginning of real growth. By acknowledging their shortcomings, the trader opens themselves up to the possibility of improvement and starts laying the foundation for long-term success.

The transition from Unconscious Incompetence to Conscious Incompetence is a crucial one. It marks the point where the trader moves from illusion to awareness. It's a difficult but necessary phase, where the trader begins to realize that true mastery of the market will take time, effort, and persistence. The journey is just beginning, and while the path ahead may be challenging, it's the only way forward for those serious about becoming successful traders.

In summary, the Unconscious Incompetence stage is characterized by enthusiasm, overconfidence, and a lack of awareness. Traders in this phase often mistake luck for skill and take on unnecessary risks without a clear plan. It's only after facing losses that they begin to realize the depth of their ignorance and the need for a more structured approach to trading. This realization is the first step toward becoming a skilled trader, and while it may be humbling, it is essential for long-term growth.

Conscious Incompetence: The Awakening of True Learning

Once a trader acknowledges that they lack the skills necessary for consistent success, they enter the second stage of development: "Conscious Incompetence." This is a pivotal phase in the trader's journey because it marks the moment where real learning begins. At this point, the trader has been humbled by the market, fully aware of their shortcomings, and is now open to growth. Gone are the days of expecting quick profits and easy wins. The trader begins to understand that mastery in trading is a long-term endeavor, one that requires patience, effort, and relentless study.

In the Conscious Incompetence phase, the trader becomes more deliberate about their education. They begin to seek out knowledge with greater intent, whether by reading trading books, enrolling in courses, or finding mentors who can guide them through the intricacies of the market. This is where the trader starts to grasp the core concepts that underpin successful trading, risk management, technical analysis, market psychology, and the importance of a structured trading plan. However, knowing these things and executing them successfully are two very different challenges.

At this stage, the trader is gathering information and beginning to build a foundation of understanding, but applying this knowledge effectively is still a major hurdle. Losses continue to occur, but unlike the earlier phase, where losses were met with confusion, they are now met with curiosity and reflection. The trader begins to ask the right questions: What went wrong?

How can I improve? Each failure becomes a stepping stone toward growth rather than a blow to their confidence.

The Gap Between Knowledge and Execution

While the Conscious Incompetence phase is filled with potential, it's also one of the most challenging. The trader now knows what they need to do to succeed, but putting that knowledge into practice proves difficult. This creates a gap between understanding and execution. They might be able to recognize a solid trade setup, but when it comes to pulling the trigger, fear and doubt creep in. Alternatively, they may find themselves chasing trades out of greed, even when their plan advises caution. These emotional obstacles become painfully clear during this phase.

For the first time, the trader recognizes the powerful influence of emotions fear, greed, impatience, and overconfidence and how they can sabotage even the best-laid plans. This emotional awareness is a critical development. In the previous stage, the trader was blissfully ignorant of how these emotions were affecting their decisions. Now, in Conscious Incompetence, they begin to see just how destructive these feelings can be to their trading outcomes. This realization can be both empowering and frustrating.

The excitement of this phase lies in the trader's active pursuit of improvement. Every book they read, every course they take, and every mistake they make adds another layer to their growing knowledge base. They feel that they're making and actually doing it are two different beasts. The trader is aware of their incompetence, and this awareness can be mentally exhausting. They see the potential for success, but they struggle to consistently implement the strategieprogress, even if their results don't yet reflect it. However, the frustration comes from the recognition that knowing what to do and actually doing it are two different beasts. The trader is aware of their incompetence, and this awareness can be mentally exhausting. They see the potential for success, but they struggle to consistently implement the strategies that would lead to it.

Persevere or Give Up

It's in the Conscious Incompetence stage that many traders choose to abandon their journey. The difficulty of trading becomes undeniable, and the harsh truth sets in: trading is much harder than they initially believed. The excitement of quick profits has long faded, replaced by the slow grind of learning from mistakes and trying to bridge the gap between knowledge and execution. It's not uncommon for traders to feel disillusioned during this phase, and many give up entirely, deciding that trading isn't for them after all.

But for those who push through, Conscious Incompetence lays the groundwork for future success. The key to advancing beyond this stage is perseverance. The trader must be willing to endure the frustration of knowing what they need to do but not always being able to do it. They must embrace mistakes, not as failures, but as valuable learning experiences that are shaping them into a better trader.

This phase is about patience and resilience. The trader must continue learning, refining their strategies, and, most importantly, practicing emotional discipline. The real growth in Conscious Incompetence comes from not just acquiring knowledge, but from learning how to manage the emotional challenges that come with trading. By staying committed to the process, traders can slowly close the gap between what they know and how they execute.

Embracing the Learning Process

Conscious Incompetence is a stage that tests a trader's resolve. It's the phase where the initial illusion of simplicity is shattered, replaced by the reality that success in trading takes time, practice, and a willingness to learn from mistakes. But it's also a phase of great potential. Traders who embrace this learning process, who commit to improving themselves both intellectually and emotionally, lay the foundation for future mastery.

This is where the real work happens. It's where traders begin to see their trading as a craft that requires constant refinement. They start to understand that losses are an inevitable part of the journey and that each mistake offers valuable lessons. Rather than being discouraged by setbacks, they begin to view them as necessary steps on the road to success.

In the Conscious Incompetence stage, traders start to shift their focus from short-term results to long-term development. They recognize that mastery won't come overnight, but that each trade, each loss, and each emotional challenge is shaping them into a more skilled and disciplined trader. The path is difficult, but for those who persevere, the rewards are worth the struggle. Every lesson learned brings them closer to the next phase of trading development, where competence starts to become a conscious and deliberate part of their approach.

Conscious Competence: The Practicing Strategist

In the third stage of development, "Conscious Competence," the trader reaches a significant milestone in their journey. No longer a novice fumbling through the markets, they've accumulated a solid foundation of knowledge. Now, they are equipped with the tools and insights necessary to execute trades with a structured plan. At this stage, the trader has a clear understanding of market behavior, technical indicators, and how to manage risk effectively. However, the journey is far from complete. Each decision they make still requires conscious thought, effort, and discipline.

With a trading system in place, the trader can identify favorable setups, plan entries and exits, and determine how much capital to risk on each trade. They've learned what works best for them through experience, trial and error, and careful analysis. However, despite having a system, vigilance remains key. The trader must stay alert, ensuring they stick to their plan and avoid slipping into bad habits or impulsive decisions.

The challenge in this phase lies in maintaining emotional control. Even though the trader knows what they need to do, emotions such as fear, greed, and impatience can still interfere with the decision-making process. For instance, they might hesitate to pull the trigger on a trade due to fear of loss or hold onto a position too long, driven by greed. These emotional triggers can disrupt an otherwise solid strategy, and overcoming them is critical to moving forward.

The Mental Toll of Conscious Trading

As the trader moves deeper into Conscious Competence, success becomes more frequent, but it's hard-earned. Consistent results are the reward for disciplined effort, but each trade requires mental energy and focus. This is a stage where the trader learns to fine-tune their craft. Every decision is deliberate, and every trade is an opportunity to learn, whether it results in profit or loss. Losses are no longer devastating but are instead seen as valuable lessons to refine their approach.

The mental toll of this phase can't be underestimated. Each trade requires careful consideration of various factors—technical signals, market conditions, and the trader's personal risk tolerance. There's no room for autopilot; each move must be intentional. The trader must remain highly focused to avoid veering off course and deviating from their strategy. This can be mentally taxing, as the trader is constantly balancing knowledge and execution, keeping emotions in check while applying learned strategies.

The pressure to perform, combined with the need for consistent discipline, makes this phase challenging. The trader is aware that they've made progress, but they also understand that there's still a long way to go. The feeling of success is tempered by the awareness that they haven't yet achieved mastery. Each step forward requires sustained effort, and even small mistakes can feel costly. This is a period of growth but also of significant mental endurance.

Trusting the Process

To move from Conscious Competence to the final stage of trading mastery, Unconscious Competence, the trader must go through a process of repetition and reinforcement. At this point, their knowledge is solid, but it hasn't yet become second nature. Advancing to the next level requires consistent practice, where the trader repeats successful actions until they no longer need to think through each step so deliberately.

This transition is about developing trust, trust in their system, in their ability to follow it, and in the long-term results it will bring. Over time, as the trader continues to execute their strategy and sees consistent results, their confidence grows. They begin to internalize the process, relying less on conscious thought and more on instinct. The mechanics of trading, identifying setups, managing risk, and executing trades, start to feel more automatic. The trader no longer needs to weigh every decision as heavily; the process starts to flow naturally.

However, getting to this point requires persistence. Mistakes are part of the journey, and the trader must learn to embrace them as opportunities for growth. Each misstep is a lesson that brings them closer to mastery. The trader must continue to refine their system, making small adjustments where necessary, and commit to the long-term process of improvement.

With continued practice, the trader will notice a shift. The market becomes more familiar, less intimidating. Patterns that once required deep analysis are now quickly recognizable. Decisions that once demanded significant mental energy start to feel intuitive. This is the beginning of Unconscious

Competence, the stage where trading becomes second nature, and the trader can operate with confidence and ease.

In the Conscious Competence stage, the trader is forging the habits, skills, and emotional resilience that will carry them into mastery. It's a phase of deliberate effort and learning, where every trade is a stepping stone toward deeper understanding and intuition. While it may be mentally exhausting at times, it's also where the trader lays the foundation for future success. With patience, practice, and perseverance, the trader will eventually reach the point where they can trust themselves and their system to navigate the market with precision.

Unconscious Competence : The Master Strategist

In the final stage, "Unconscious Competence" , the trader achieves the ultimate level of mastery. After years of dedicated practice, study, and experience, trading has become second nature. At this stage, the trader no longer needs to consciously analyze every step of their process. Instead, their decision-making flows effortlessly, rooted in a deep understanding of the markets and their personal trading system.

The trader moves through the market with calm, unshakable confidence. They trust in their strategy and execute their trades with precision, free from the hesitation that once marked earlier stages. While they remain aware of risk and continue to follow their plan, they do so with a quiet assurance, having already internalized the principles that guide their approach. The focus that was once required to analyze every trade is now instinctual, allowing the trader to navigate the markets with an ease that only comes with time and experience.

Intuitive Market Understanding and Emotional Mastery

In "Unconscious Competence" , the trader's understanding of the market has evolved to an almost intuitive level. They can quickly recognize patterns, setups, and shifts in sentiment, allowing them to make decisions swiftly and confidently. What once took significant effort to analyze is now effortlessly processed. The trader doesn't just follow the market,, they anticipate it, often sensing opportunities before they fully develop. Their years of experience have honed their ability to see beyond the surface, making quick, accurate assessments based on the subtlest of cues.

What separates this stage from earlier ones is not just technical skill but also emotional mastery. Fear, greed, and impatience no longer have power over the trader's decisions. While emotions are always present, they are managed with ease. A loss is no longer a source of frustration or anxiety, it's simply part of the process. Likewise, a win is not something to get overly excited about. The trader maintains a balanced mindset, treating both wins and losses with the same level of detachment. This emotional equilibrium allows them to stay composed, even when the market becomes volatile or unpredictable.

At this stage, the trader doesn't attach themselves to individual trades. They understand that no single trade defines their success. Instead, they are focused on the bigger picture, knowing that their long-term consistency and discipline are what drive their success. This mindset allows them to remain flexible, adjusting their strategy when necessary but always staying true to their core principles.

The Strategic Thinker

In "Unconscious Competence", the trader evolves into a true strategist. No longer reacting to the market's moves, they are instead proactively thinking ahead, anticipating various scenarios and preparing for multiple outcomes. Their deep understanding of both the market and their own trading system allows them to adjust their approach with confidence. When market conditions shift, they don't panic. Instead, they adapt, knowing that their strategy will stand the test of time as long as they maintain their discipline.

This strategic mindset is what sets master traders apart. They aren't just looking for the next opportunity; they're thinking several steps ahead, ready to adjust their game plan as needed. This ability to think in scenarios and prepare for various outcomes gives them an edge over less experienced traders, who may still be reacting emotionally or struggling to stick to a plan.

Mastery is a Journey, Not a Destination

It's important to note that "Unconscious Competence" doesn't mean the trader has nothing left to learn. Markets are constantly evolving, and even the most experienced traders need to stay sharp. However, at this stage, learning and adaptation are part of the natural rhythm of their process. The trader can make adjustments and evolve their strategy without overthinking or second-guessing themselves. They trust their intuition, knowing that it's been shaped by years of experience and study.

This level of competence also comes with the understanding that mastery is not a final destination it's a continuous journey. The markets will always present new challenges, and the trader must remain committed to improvement, even after reaching the pinnacle of their skill. However, this ongoing learning no longer feels burdensome. Instead, it's a natural extension of the trader's passion for the craft, driven by a deep desire to remain at the top of their game.

Effortless Expertise

Reaching "Unconscious Competence" is the goal for every trader, but it's a journey that takes years of dedication. It requires countless hours of study, practice, and reflection, along with the ability to persevere through setbacks and mistakes. For those who achieve it, trading becomes a seamless, intuitive process. The trader moves through the markets with expertise, navigating complex conditions with ease, and executing trades with unwavering discipline and confidence.

This is the level of mastery that few traders ever reach. It represents the culmination of all the lessons learned, all the hours spent refining their craft, and all the emotional battles fought along the way. At this stage, trading is no longer a struggle, it's a natural expression of the trader's deep understanding of both the market and themselves.

In "Unconscious Competence" , the trader embodies the ultimate goal: to move through the markets with expertise, precision, and grace, achieving success through consistent, effortless execution.

Chapter 12

Mastering the Craft: Developing Skills Through Consistent, Focused Practice

In trading, as in any discipline, mastery is built through deliberate training. This chapter breaks down the process of developing the mindset, habits, and routines necessary to transform theory into skill. From refining technical abilities to cultivating emotional resilience, we explore how structured training helps traders turn knowledge into instinct and elevate their performance to the next level.

Actionable Steps: How to Train as a Master Strategist

Mastering the art of trading requires more than just theory. it demands a structured, actionable approach to learning and improvement. Success in trading, much like any other discipline, stems from consistent practice, analysis, and refinement. Here, we'll break down the training process into six key steps: spotting, tracking, measuring, coming up with a solution, implementing it, and measuring again before repeating the cycle. This approach ensures that you continually grow and improve your strategy, making you more adaptable and effective as a trader.

Step 1: Spotting: Identifying Patterns and Problems

The first step to improving as a trader is spotting patterns and identifying problems in your trading approach. This means recognizing both the things you're doing well and the areas where you may be falling short. This isn't just about looking for market patterns, though that's a big part of it, it's also about understanding your own habits and behaviors.

For example, do you find yourself consistently entering trades too early or too late? Are you sticking to your strategy, or are you letting emotions drive your decisions? Start by reviewing your recent trades. Look for recurring mistakes or missed opportunities. Spotting is about recognizing trends in your behavior, strategy, and the market.

behavior, strategy, and the market.

Actionable Tip: Keep a detailed trading journal. Record every trade, noting what led you to enter or exit the position, how you felt during the trade, and what the outcome was. Review this journal regularly to spot recurring patterns or issues.

Step 2: Tracking: Monitoring Your Performance

Once you've identified a potential problem or pattern, the next step is to track it over time. It's one thing to notice that you tend to hold onto losing trades too long, but it's another to quantify how often this happens and how much it's costing you. Tracking helps you build a data-driven understanding of your strengths and weaknesses.

Begin by selecting key metrics to monitor. These could include your win/loss ratio, average time in trades, risk/reward ratio, or the percentage of your trades that follow your strategy. Tracking these metrics over time will give you a clear picture of where you need to improve.

Actionable Tip: Use a spreadsheet or trading platform that allows you to track your performance. Focus on a few key metrics that are most relevant to your trading strategy and goals. For example, if you struggle with managing risk, track how often you follow your stop-loss rules.

Step 3: Measuring: Analyzing the Data

Tracking your performance gives you data, but it's the analysis of that data that leads to insights. Once you've gathered enough information, the next step is to measure how well you're doing relative to your goals. This involves looking at your tracked data objectively and asking key questions:

- What patterns are emerging in my trading?
- Are my trades following my strategy, or am I deviating?
- What impact are my emotional decisions having on my profitability?

Measuring is about looking for cause and effect. For instance, if you notice that your win rate is high when you trade within your strategy but significantly lower when you deviate from it, that's an important insight. It shows you that discipline is a key factor in your success.

Actionable Tip:
Schedule regular performance reviews, weekly, monthly, or quarterly. During these reviews, measure your performance against your goals. Identify what's working well and what needs improvement.

Step 4: Coming Up with a Solution: Crafting a Plan for Improvement

Once you've measured your performance and identified areas for improvement, the next step is to come up with a solution. This is where you start developing a plan to address the problems you've spotted and tracked. If you're consistently losing money on trades because you exit too early, what can you do to stay in trades longer? If emotions are leading you to break your strategy, how can you control them?

The key here is to be specific. Rather than saying, "I'll be more disciplined," come up with concrete actions you can take to improve. For example, you might decide to set stricter stop-loss and take-profit points to remove emotion from the decision-making process.

Actionable Tip:
Write down your solutions as part of your trading plan. For every problem you've identified, come up with at least one specific, actionable step you can take to address it. Make sure these steps are realistic and measurable.

Step 5: Implementing the Solution – Putting Your Plan into Action

Coming up with a solution is just the beginning, what matters is how well you implement it. The implementation phase is where you put your plan into action and test it in real trading conditions. This is the stage where you actively work to change your habits, improve your strategies, and become a better trader.

The key to successful implementation is discipline. Stick to the plan you've created, even when emotions might tempt you to deviate. If your solution involves waiting for a better entry point, practice patience. If it involves cutting losses quicker, follow through without hesitation. The market will provide plenty of opportunities to test your solution, so be prepared to stick with it.

Actionable Tip:
Start small. If you're implementing a new solution, test it with smaller trades before applying it to larger positions. This way, you can see how it works without risking too much capital.

Step 6: Measuring Again: Evaluating the Results

Once you've implemented your solution, the next step is to measure the results. Did your solution work? Are you seeing improvement in the areas you targeted? Just like in Step 3, this stage involves analyzing your performance data, but now you're specifically looking to see if your changes are having the desired effect.

Sometimes, a solution will work perfectly, and you'll see immediate improvements in your trading. Other times, the solution may not have the effect you expected, and you'll need to go back to the drawing board. This is all part of the process of continuous improvement.

Actionable Tip:
After a few weeks or months of implementing your solution, review your tracked data and compare it to your performance before you made the change. Look for improvements in the specific areas you were targeting, and decide whether the solution is worth keeping.

Repeat the Cycle: Continuous Improvement

The final step in this process is to repeat the cycle. Trading is an ever-evolving discipline, and even once you've fixed one problem, new challenges will emerge. The goal is to make continuous improvement a habit. Spot, track, measure, solve, implement, and measure again. With each cycle, you'll get closer to becoming a master strategist.

As you repeat this process, you'll also start to develop a deeper understanding of the market and your own trading tendencies. This cycle of improvement will not only make you a more disciplined trader but also a more adaptable and insightful one.

Actionable Tip:
Embrace the process of repetition. Don't rush the training cycle, each step is important. Take time to refine your strategies and solutions with each pass through the cycle. Keep a long-term perspective and focus on progress rather than perfection.

Embrace Structured Training

Becoming a master strategist in trading requires a structured, actionable approach to continuous improvement. By following these six steps spotting, tracking, measuring, coming up with a solution, implementing it, and measuring again, you create a repeatable cycle of growth that sharpens your skills and strengthens your discipline. This approach not only helps you fine-tune your strategies but also instills the habits necessary for long-term success in the ever-changing world of trading.

Part 5

Beyond profits : Seeing the Big Picture

Trading is like weaving a tapestry, up close, it's a chaotic blend of wins and losses. But step back, and a grand design emerges. Beyond individual trades, the real success lies in your strategy, the process, and the bigger vision. Shifting focus from short-term gains to the long-term journey transforms profits into just one piece of the larger story: the evolution of a true strategist.

Chapter 13

Three Months, Not One Trade:
The Long Game

In the journey to becoming a master strategist, a key shift occurs in how traders perceive time. Most novice traders obsess over single trades, treating each one as if it will define their success. This mindset not only traps them in short-term thinking but also magnifies emotional reactions to every win or loss. A master strategist, however, does not trade for the immediate outcome, they trade for the larger arc, focusing on a much broader horizon. In this chapter, we move from the micro-view of individual trades to a long-term perspective: focusing on the results of a three-month cycle, rather than obsessing over any one trade.

The Danger of Short-Term Thinking

The allure of trading lies in the potential for quick gains, but this same allure traps traders in a vicious cycle. When traders focus on one trade at a time, they are often driven by emotion, fear of missing out, greed when a position goes in their favor, or panic when the market moves against them. In this reactive mindset, every trade feels like it must succeed, and losses feel catastrophic. But in reality, a single trade is only one of many in a long series.

When you zero in on the results of one trade, you amplify the emotional stakes. You might celebrate a win as if you've cracked the market's code, or despair over a loss as if it defines your entire strategy. But success in trading is never about one trade. It's about the cumulative result of dozens, if not hundreds, of decisions over a significant period. That's why the mindset of the master strategist shifts from trading for immediate success to trading with a broader timeframe in mind.

The master strategist knows that a single trade doesn't make or break a strategy. The real game is in the consistent execution of a proven system over time. A loss isn't a setback, it's part of the process. A win isn't a signal to relax, it's part of the cycle. Each trade contributes to the bigger picture, and that bigger picture reveals itself over the course of several months, not hours or days.

The Power of a Three-Month Perspective

Focusing on a three-month cycle, rather than the outcome of a single trade, offers several advantages that transform the way you approach trading. The first advantage is emotional distance. When you trade with a long-term view, individual outcomes don't carry as much weight. You're able to approach each trade objectively, knowing that it's part of a larger sample size. You've already accepted that some trades will fail, but you also know that, over time, your strategy will yield a net gain.

The second advantage is that a three-month horizon allows for strategic adjustments. Rather than making knee-jerk reactions to a losing streak or an unexpected market move, you can assess your performance over a longer timeframe and make informed decisions based on a comprehensive review of data. You begin to see trends in your own trading behavior, as well as in the market, that aren't visible when you focus too closely on short-term results.

By embracing a three-month perspective, the master strategist shifts from a mindset of immediacy to one of patience and consistency. You stop chasing every opportunity and start looking for the patterns that repeat over time. This helps you trust your system, even during rough patches, and avoid the impulsive decisions that short-term thinking breeds.

The Emotional Balance of Long-Term Trading

One of the greatest benefits of adopting a three-month approach is the emotional control it fosters. In earlier stages of trading, emotions like fear and greed dominate your decision-making. In the "Conscious Competence" stage, as we discussed, traders battle their emotions daily, working to stick to their plan despite the ups and downs. But as you focus on a broader horizon, emotional triggers lose their power.

When you evaluate your performance over several months rather than in real-time, you can take a more analytical view of your trades. Losses are no longer devastating, because they're not standalone events, they're part of a system. You're able to see how losses fit into the overall strategy and recognize that they're just the cost of doing business. Wins, while satisfying, are also just a part of the bigger cycle.

This long-term view reduces the emotional spikes that come with every trade. Instead of riding the highs and lows, you maintain a steady, even keel, focused on executing your plan rather than reacting to every market move. You become less attached to individual trades and more committed to the process as a whole.

Tracking Progress Over Three Months

A vital part of maintaining a long-term mindset is tracking your progress over three months. This isn't just about tracking your profits and losses; it's about evaluating the effectiveness of your system, your emotional discipline, and your decision-making. At the end of each quarter, you should take time to review your trades in detail, looking for patterns that can inform your next three-month cycle.

Did you stick to your plan, or did emotions lead you to deviate? Were there certain market conditions that consistently led to losses, and if so, can you adjust your system to account for them? Did you execute your trades with discipline, or did you fall into bad habits?

By analyzing your performance over a three-month period, you gain valuable insights that you can use to improve your system, strengthen your emotional control, and continue your progress as a master strategist.

A Long-Term Habit

Developing a three-month mindset isn't just about shifting your focus in trading, it's about creating a habit of long-term thinking that extends beyond the markets. It teaches you to value consistency over quick wins, and to embrace patience and discipline as the true markers of success. The three-month horizon allows you to see the market and your role in it, as part of a larger process, one that requires foresight, strategy, and resilience.

This shift in perspective is what separates successful traders from those who remain stuck in short-term thinking. It's the difference between reacting to the market and mastering it. The three-month mindset helps you stay grounded, focused, and consistently moving toward your goal.

As you move from trade-to-trade thinking to a broader three-month approach, you start to see trading for what it truly is: a long-term game of strategy, patience, and discipline. No single trade defines you, and no individual loss or win determines your success. It's the cumulative effect of every decision, every adjustment, and every lesson learned that brings you closer to becoming a master strategist. By focusing on three months, you free yourself from the emotional rollercoaster of short-term trading and position yourself for sustained success over the long haul.

Chapter 14

The Checklist: Turning Complexity into Simplicity

Trading, at its core, is a game of probabilities. But while the market may be unpredictable, your actions don't have to be. For the master strategist, preparation is everything. A solid trading system, no matter how refined, is nothing without the discipline to follow it consistently. And this is where "the checklist" comes in, a simple, yet profoundly powerful tool that brings structure to the chaos, ensures discipline in execution, and reduces the influence of emotions.

The Power of Routine in Chaos

It might sound counterintuitive, but trading thrives on routine. The market is chaotic, fluctuating on news, sentiment, and countless unseen forces. As a trader, you cannot control the market, but you can control how you react to it. A checklist is your shield against the emotional swings that derail so many traders. It grounds you, pulling you back to your strategy when fear or greed whispers in your ear to abandon it.

Imagine you're in the heat of the moment: the market has moved sharply, and you're faced with a decision to either enter or exit a trade. Your mind is racing, emotions are swirling, and second-guessing begins to creep in. Without a system, you might act impulsively, deviating from your plan. But with a checklist? You have a clear process to follow. It acts as a safeguard, guiding you through each step with calm precision.

The master strategist doesn't leave decisions to chance or gut feelings. They rely on a set of predetermined criteria that have been proven to work over time. This checklist is their roadmap, leading them through each trade with consistency, no matter the market conditions.

Building Your Strategic Checklist

Your checklist is more than a to-do list, it's the embodiment of your trading philosophy, distilled into actionable steps. Crafting the right checklist requires thought and intention, as each step should align with your overall strategy and goals. Let's break down how to build this vital tool.

1. Pre-Trade Preparation

Every successful trade starts before you even look at the charts. The first section of your checklist should focus on "preparation". This ensures you are entering the market with a clear head, the necessary information, and a solid understanding of what you are trying to achieve.

"Check your mindset" : Are you in the right mental space to trade today? If you're stressed, distracted, or overly emotional, step away. Trading requires clarity, and your emotional state plays a huge role in decision-making.
"Review the news" : Any significant news or economic events that could impact the markets today? This includes earnings reports, geopolitical events, or central bank announcements.
"Double-check your strategy" : Are you trading within your system's parameters? Review your strategy before you even think about executing a trade.

This pre-trade phase is all about setting the stage, ensuring that you are emotionally stable, fully informed, and prepared to execute your plan.

2. The Setup: Identifying Opportunities

Next on your checklist is the process of "identifying trading opportunities". These are the signals or setups that you've learned to recognize and trust. But before jumping in, it's crucial to make sure that the setup meets all of your criteria. This is where most traders fall short, they see an opportunity, but it only checks a few boxes, not all of them.

Confirm technical signals : Are all your technical indicators aligned? Whether it's moving averages, trend lines, or support/resistance levels, your setup should meet all of your conditions before moving forward.
Check the market environment : Is the market trending or consolidating? Ensure that your setup fits the current market conditions. Trading in a range-bound market with a trend-following strategy will lead to poor results.
Review risk/reward ratio : Is the trade worth the risk? Calculate your risk/reward before entering. If the potential reward doesn't justify the risk, skip the trade.

This section of the checklist helps you avoid the trap of taking trades that don't fully meet your criteria. It enforces patience and discipline, ensuring that you only act on high-probability setups.

3. Execution: Pulling the Trigger

Once you've identified a valid setup, it's time to execute, but execution is more than just entering the trade. This part of your checklist ensures that you do so with precision and without hesitation.

"Set your stop-loss" : Before you enter, determine where your stop-loss will be placed. This is the price at which you will exit the trade if it moves against you. It's your first line of defense.
"Define your profit target" : Decide in advance where you'll take profits. This keeps you from getting greedy or closing the trade too early.
"Size your position" : How much capital are you willing to risk on this trade? Make sure you're adhering to your risk management rules, which should typically limit risk to a small percentage of your overall account.

Executing a trade is often where emotions run high, but a checklist keeps you grounded. It allows you to enter the market with a clear plan, minimizing the chances of impulsive actions.

4. Managing the Trade

Once a trade is open, emotions like fear and greed can intensify, especially as the market fluctuates. This is where the next part of your checklist comes into play: "trade management" .

"Follow your plan": Stick to your stop-loss and profit target. Don't adjust them out of fear or hope unless there's a solid technical reason to do so.
"Monitor without micromanaging": Keep an eye on the trade,

5. Post-Trade Reflection

Every trade, win or lose, is a learning opportunity. The final part of your checklist focuses on "post-trade analysis".

"Log the trade" : Record the details of the trade, including the setup, entry, stop-loss, target, and outcome. This information will be invaluable for reviewing your performance over time.
"Review your emotional state" : Were you calm and focused during the trade, or did emotions influence your decisions? This self-awareness is key to improving your trading psychology.
"Evaluate the result" : Did the trade follow your plan, and did it meet your expectations? If not, what can you learn from it?

Post-trade reflection is a critical part of long-term success. It allows you to learn from both your mistakes and your successes, continually improving your system and your discipline.

The Checklist as a Discipline Tool

A well-constructed checklist does more than just guide you through the mechanics of trading, it instills discipline. Every time you follow the checklist, you're reinforcing the habits of a master strategist. The checklist removes the uncertainty and emotions from decision-making, allowing you to execute your trades with consistency and confidence.

In the heat of trading, when emotions run high, the checklist is your anchor. It keeps you grounded in logic and reason, helping you to stick to your plan even when the market throws curveballs.

The Habit of Mastery

In "Becoming a Master Strategist", the checklist is not just a tool, it's a mindset. It represents the transition from reactive trading to proactive, calculated action. It forces you to slow down, follow a system, and treat trading as the strategic game it is, not a rush for quick gains.

The master strategist doesn't trade from instinct alone. They trade from a position of preparation, discipline, and structured thinking. With your checklist in hand, you're no longer guessing, you're executing a proven system that aligns with your long-term goals. This is how mastery is built, one trade at a time, with a plan and a process that keeps you focused on the bigger picture.

Chapter 15

The Shadow Mentor: Coaching Yourself from the Third Perspective

In every great journey, there comes a time when the hero must confront their own reflection, not just the face they show the world, but the one that lies hidden deep within. To become a master strategist, you must learn to separate from yourself and observe your actions as if you were an outsider, a shadow walking beside you. This is the art of "self-coaching from the third perspective" . You become both the player and the mentor, the strategist and the observer.

Awakening the Shadow Mentor

Close your eyes for a moment. Imagine standing at the edge of a battlefield, but instead of charging in, you pause. You take a step back, then another, until you're no longer in the heat of the battle. Instead, you're watching yourself, your moves, your decisions, your hesitations. This is the power of the "Shadow Mentor" . It's the version of you that exists outside of your emotions, beyond the immediate pressure of the market, seeing everything from an elevated, detached view.

In trading, this skill is crucial. When you're deep in the flow, it's easy to become consumed by the pulse of the market, your thoughts, your feelings, your impulses. But the true strategist knows that the path to mastery is in "learning to coach yourself" . You must become your own mentor, constantly assessing, adjusting, and refining.

But how? The first step is learning to step outside of yourself, to see yourself as both the player and the strategist guiding the game. The moment you learn to coach yourself from this third perspective, you unlock a new layer of insight.

Becoming the Observer: Training Your Shadow Vision

The art of shadow mentoring begins with a simple question: "What would I say to myself if I were not me?" In the heat of battle, this question separates the reactive trader from the strategic one. It pulls you out of the chaos of the moment and into a space of clarity.

Imagine a scenario where you've just made a bad trade. Your emotions flare, frustration clouds your mind, and you're tempted to act out of impulse. Now, pause. Imagine you're watching yourself as if you were a spectator, observing the move from a distance. What advice would you give yourself if you weren't in the driver's seat?

This mental shift is key. It allows you to assess your actions without judgment, as if you were coaching another person. With each decision, you become both the actor and the analyst. You critique not to punish but to guide. This process sharpens your mind, transforming losses into lessons and victories into affirmations.

This is how a master strategist trains: not just through repetition, but by cultivating the ability to observe themselves with the cold, calculated clarity of an outsider.

Embracing Duality: The Hero and the Guide

In every great story, there's always a mentor, a guide who pushes the hero beyond their limits. But what happens when you must become your own guide? The greatest traders know this secret: "you must split yourself into two, one who plays the game and one who coaches the player."

The duality is challenging at first. It feels unnatural to pull yourself out of the action, especially when emotions run high.

But as you practice, you begin to feel the power in it. You start to recognize patterns not only in the market but in yourself, your tendencies, your strengths, and, most importantly, your weaknesses.

The shadow mentor isn't harsh; it's patient. It's the version of you that sees the bigger picture, reminding you of the long game when you're tempted to react to short-term fluctuations. It's the voice in your head that says, "This is not about the trade in front of you, it's about the next hundred trades."

The Mirror Test: Reflecting Without Judgment

One of the most powerful tools in self-coaching is the "mirror test" . This is the act of reflecting on your trades as if you were analyzing someone else's performance. After every trade, win or lose, sit down and dissect it from the perspective of a mentor. Ask yourself:

- What did I do well?
- Where did I falter?
- What could I have done differently?
- What emotions were driving my decisions?

But here's the key: "no judgment" . You are not your mistakes. You are not your wins. You are a strategist in the making, constantly evolving. The mirror test is not about assigning blame, it's about gathering insight. The more you engage in this reflection, the more your shadow mentor strengthens, guiding you with precision in future trades.

The Shadow Mentor's Voice: Building Inner Dialogue

In the deepest moments of doubt, when the market has knocked you down, it's easy to lose sight of the bigger picture. But this is when the shadow mentor speaks the loudest. "It's the quiet voice of reason", reminding you that one loss does not define you, that the path to mastery is paved with setbacks.

In trading, your greatest asset is your inner dialogue. How you speak to yourself after a trade, especially a loss, determines your ability to bounce back. The shadow mentor isn't harsh; it doesn't scold you for making mistakes. Instead, it asks, "What did you learn from this?"

Every mistake is an opportunity to improve. Every misstep is a chance to sharpen your strategy. The shadow mentor doesn't dwell on the past, it uses the past as fuel for the future.

Strategizing in Silence: The Power of Reflection

One of the greatest lessons in coaching yourself is the value of "silence". In the chaos of the market, silence becomes a sanctuary. After each trading session, take time to step back. Not to analyze the market, but to analyze yourself.

In the silence, you hear the whispers of your shadow mentor. You can feel the subtle shifts in your thought process, notice the patterns in your behavior, and recognize the emotional triggers that often go unnoticed in the heat of battle.

This practice isn't just about becoming a better trader, it's about becoming more self-aware. The better you know yourself, the better you can coach yourself.

Leveling Up: Your Shadow Mentor Evolves

As you continue down the path of mastery, you'll notice something interesting: "your shadow mentor evolves with you". The insights that once seemed distant become second nature. What was once a deliberate effort to coach yourself from the third perspective becomes automatic.
As you continue down the path of mastery, you'll notice something interesting: "your shadow mentor evolves with you". The insights that once seemed distant become second nature. What was once a deliberate effort to coach yourself from the third perspective becomes automatic.

Over time, you'll find that the shadow mentor's voice becomes a steady guide, always there, always watching. And in moments of uncertainty, when the market throws its fiercest storms at you, it will be your anchor. It will remind you that every decision is part of a larger strategy, every loss a necessary lesson, every win a stepping stone to something greater.
Over time, you'll find that the shadow mentor's voice becomes a steady guide, always there, always watching. And in moments of uncertainty, when the market throws its fiercest storms at you, it will be your anchor. It will remind you that every decision is part of a larger strategy, every loss a necessary lesson, every win a stepping stone to something greater.

Final Lesson of the Shadow Mentor

In the end, coaching yourself from the third perspective isn't just a technique, it's a way of thinking. It's a mindset that allows you to separate from the noise, to see clearly when the path is clouded, and to trust in your ability to guide yourself.

As you step into each new trading day, remember this:" You are both the player and the mentor, the strategist and the student." And the moment you can observe yourself with clarity, without judgment, you unlock the power of true mastery.

In the world of trading, the game is long, and the battles are many. But with your shadow mentor by your side, guiding your every move, there is no challenge too great, no setback too daunting. You are a strategist in the making, and with each step, you come closer to the ultimate victory, not just in trading, but in mastering yourself.

Part 6

The Lazy Couch: Strategic Rest

In the relentless pursuit of success, traders often forget one critical aspect of mastery, rest. It's tempting to think that progress comes only from constant action, but in truth, true growth often happens in the quiet moments, the spaces between. The Lazy Couch isn't about complacency or giving up; it's about creating a sanctuary where the mind can recover, reflect, and recalibrate. This is where real breakthroughs occur.

Chapter 16
The Silent Weapon : The Mind Needs Rest

Every strategist knows that the greatest weapon is not forged in battle but in the quiet moments between. When the market is silent, and the charts have dimmed, the real battle begins. "Rest" is the silent weapon of the master strategist, and yet, it's often the most overlooked.

In trading, the temptation is always to push forward, to outwork, to obsess over every move. But the truth is, the sharpest minds are not those constantly in motion; they are the ones that understand the power of stillness, of stepping back and letting the mind breathe.

Just as a warrior sharpens their sword between battles, a trader must sharpen their mind through intentional periods of rest. This is not a sign of weakness, on the contrary, it is a display of wisdom and discipline. The mind, like any instrument, needs time to recharge, recalibrate, and realign.

The Strategist's Dilemma: The Fear of Rest

The greatest enemy of rest is fear, the fear that stepping away will cause you to miss something crucial. The fear that the market will move without you, leaving you behind. This is the dilemma every trader faces: balancing the need for constant vigilance with the need for mental rejuvenation.

In the heat of trading, it's easy to fall into the trap of overanalysis, obsessing over every tick, every fluctuation. The adrenaline keeps you alert, but over time, it dulls your edge. What many traders fail to realize is that "the mind, much like the market, operates in cycles" . There are times to push, to strategize, to execute, and there are times to withdraw, reflect, and recover.

The mind, when fatigued, becomes a poor decision-maker. It reacts rather than responds, and a trader who operates in a state of constant mental exhaustion is one prone to errors, impulsive trades, misjudgments, and emotional decision-making.

The Art of Strategic Withdrawal

Great strategists know when to advance, but more importantly, they know when to retreat. "Strategic withdrawal" is the art of pulling back not out of defeat, but out of wisdom. In trading, this means knowing when to close the charts, walk away from the screen, and allow your mind to reset.

Rest is not a luxury; it's a necessity. It's the space where clarity is born, where the noise of the market fades, and your subconscious can process the lessons learned. It's during these periods of stillness that insights often emerge, ideas solidify, and strategies crystallize.

Think of rest as the space between notes in a song. Without it, the melody becomes chaotic, indistinguishable. It's the pauses that give the music meaning, just as it is the moments of rest that give your trading decisions purpose.

Rest is Strategy

There's a reason why professional athletes have rest days, why artists step away from their work, and why great minds in history embraced solitude. "Rest is strategy" . It's the deliberate act of giving your mind the space to regenerate, so that when you return, you return sharper, more focused, and more in tune with the market's rhythm.

In trading, the market can feel like a relentless storm, but no storm lasts forever. And no storm can be weathered without moments of shelter. Rest is your shelter. It's where you regain your strength, reset your perspective, and rediscover your strategic edge.

Rewiring the Mind Through Rest

The mind is a complex machine, constantly taking in data, analyzing patterns, and making decisions. But like any machine, it needs downtime to operate at its best. When you rest, your brain doesn't stop working, it processes information differently. It integrates what you've learned, creates new neural pathways, and strengthens your decision-making abilities.

Think of the moments where you've had a sudden flash of insight or clarity, not while staring at a chart but perhaps while walking, meditating, or even in the middle of the night. These are the moments where your rested mind is revealing its work. "This is the mind's way of telling you that rest is part of the process".

Rest is not idle time. It's a critical component of your growth as a strategist. Without it, your progress is stunted, your learning is incomplete, and your decisions become increasingly reactive rather than proactive.

Trusting the Process

One of the hardest lessons for a trader is to trust the process, especially when that process includes stepping away. But this is what separates the amateur from the master strategist. The amateur thinks that rest is lost time, that the more time they spend staring at the screen, the better trader they will become. The master strategist knows that rest is the secret ingredient to longevity.

There will always be another trade, another opportunity, another move in the market. But your mind is finite. Without rest, you burn through your mental capital faster than any financial loss could ever do. Trusting the process means trusting that rest is not only necessary but integral to your long-term success.

The Strategist's Cycle: Effort and Rest

In every story, the hero doesn't just fight battle after battle without reprieve. They take time to heal, to train, to reflect on their journey before returning stronger. You, too, are on a hero's journey in the world of trading, and "the hero's cycle" is one of effort and rest.

After every trading session, allow yourself time to recover. This is where the real growth happens. It's in the moments away from the screen that your mind sharpens its skills, internalizes its lessons, and prepares for the next battle.

Embracing Stillness: The Quiet Edge

In the fast-paced world of trading, the idea of stillness may seem counterintuitive. But stillness is where your edge lies. It's the place where you can hear the quiet whispers of your intuition, unclouded by the noise of the market. It's where your mind can breathe, recalibrate, and regain its clarity.

There will always be another trade, another opportunity, another move in the market. But your mind is finite. Without rest, you burn through your mental capital faster than any financial loss could ever do. Trusting the process means trusting that rest is not only necessary but integral to your long-term success.

The Strategist's Cycle: Effort and Rest

In every story, the hero doesn't just fight battle after battle without reprieve. They take time to heal, to train, to reflect on their journey before returning stronger. You, too, are on a hero's journey in the world of trading, and "the hero's cycle" is one of effort and rest.

After every trading session, allow yourself time to recover. This is where the real growth happens. It's in the moments away from the screen that your mind sharpens its skills, internalizes its lessons, and prepares for the next battle.

Embracing Stillness: The Quiet Edge

In the fast-paced world of trading, the idea of stillness may seem counterintuitive. But stillness is where your edge lies. It's the place where you can hear the quiet whispers of your intuition, unclouded by the noise of the market. It's where your mind can breathe, recalibrate, and regain its clarity.

Stillness is not about doing nothing; it's about "being present" in the absence of action. It's where the greatest insights often emerge, where strategies that once felt distant suddenly become clear. When you embrace stillness, you give yourself the gift of perspective.

Resting with Intention

Rest is most powerful when done with intention. It's not about mindlessly scrolling through distractions or numbing your mind with noise. It's about finding activities that recharge you, whether that's spending time in nature, meditating, exercising, or simply sitting in silence.

Intentional rest is about creating space for your mind to wander, to explore new ideas, and to digest the lessons of the market. It's about stepping away with purpose, knowing that in doing so, you are preparing for your next strategic move.

The Final Lesson: Rest is Mastery

In the end, the mind that rests is the mind that wins. "Rest is mastery". It's the unseen force that powers your decisions, sharpens your instincts, and strengthens your resolve. It's the place where the strategist is born, not in the heat of battle, but in the quiet moments in between.

As a master strategist, your greatest tool is not your knowledge of the market, nor your ability to analyze charts. It's your understanding of the mind's need for rest, and your willingness to embrace it as part of your strategy.

Rest, recharge, and return. The battle is long, but with rest, you are always prepared for the next move.

Chapter 17

The Aha Moment: Clarity in Stillness

In the quiet corners of the mind, where thoughts float like leaves on a still pond, an epiphany emerges, sudden, sharp, and crystal clear. It's the "aha moment" , the flash of understanding that cuts through the fog of uncertainty and brings everything into focus. But this moment doesn't come from overworking, grinding, or relentless pursuit. It comes from rest, from giving the mind space to breathe, and from letting the subconscious unravel the mysteries we don't even know we're pondering.

The "aha moment" is not an accident. It's a reward, a byproduct of aligning with the deeper currents of thought. After the long hours of effort and concentration, it's in the moments of stillness where clarity strikes. Rest isn't just recovery; it's where connections are made, ideas solidify, and new possibilities reveal themselves. This is where the master strategist pulls ahead, not by sheer force of will, but by learning the art of stepping back and letting the mind work behind the scenes.

The Power of Letting Go

In trading, much like life, the instinct is often to control every detail, to hold the reins tightly and force a solution. But the truth is, some answers only reveal themselves when you let go. The market is a beast, always in motion, always fluctuating. It's easy to think you need to be on top of every tick, every shift, but the reality is the opposite.

When you rest, your mind enters a different mode, one that isn't cluttered with the noise of analysis or decision-making. It becomes free to wander, to explore, and to solve problems from a fresh angle. This is where the "aha moments" are born, in that strange space where you've given up on finding the answer, and suddenly, there it is, waiting for you.

The master strategist knows this. They don't force insight; they create the conditions for it to flourish. Like the calm before a storm, these moments of rest are where the mind gathers its energy, its perspective, and its understanding, waiting to strike with precision.

Unconscious Processing: The Secret Engine

While the conscious mind is obsessed with facts, figures, and logic, the unconscious mind works in the background, weaving together strands of information in ways the conscious mind can't grasp. When you rest, this unconscious engine kicks into high gear, processing everything you've absorbed the charts you've studied, the trades you've made, the lessons you've learned.

It's during this downtime, when you've stepped away from the charts, that the brain makes connections, drawing lines between seemingly unrelated pieces of data. Suddenly, a pattern emerges, a strategy clicks into place, and you understand something you didn't before. This is the magic of the "aha moment", a gift from your own mind when you least expect it.

This process is why rest isn't just important; it's critical. Without it, you deny yourself the deeper insights that could change the way you approach the market. You're left stuck in a loop of surface-level thinking, chasing short-term gains but missing the bigger picture that's hiding just beneath the surface.

The Moment of Illumination

In every story , there's a moment where the hero, after being beaten down and pushed to their limits, suddenly rises with new resolve, new clarity. Their eyes sharpen, their stance shifts, and everything becomes crystal clear. The enemy, once overwhelming, now seems predictable, almost transparent. They see the path to victory where before there was only confusion. This is the "aha moment", a sudden burst of insight that changes the entire game.

For traders, this is no different. After the grind of studying, testing, and refining, there comes a time where the pieces fall into place. You see the market not just as a series of random movements, but as a living organism with patterns, flow and rhythms. Your strategy, once rigid and mechanical, becomes fluid, adaptable, and responsive. You no longer chase trades; you anticipate them. You no longer react; you predict.

And just like that, you've unlocked a new level of understanding.

Training Your Mind for Insight

Here's the secret to the "aha moment" : it doesn't just happen by chance. It's the result of consistent mental training, of pushing yourself and then stepping back. Like a master martial artist who trains relentlessly but knows the value of meditation, you must condition your mind to handle both the intensity of the market and the serenity of rest.

The more you practice this balance, the more frequently those moments of clarity will come. You'll start to see patterns faster, react more calmly, and understand the market with a depth you didn't have before. This isn't just skill; it's intuition sharpened by rest and reflection.

But it's also patience. The "aha moment" can't be rushed. It arrives when you're ready for it, when you've put in the work but also when you've given yourself permission to stop working. This delicate balance is what separates the good traders from the great ones.

Beyond the Epiphany

The "aha moment" is not the end; it's a turning point. It doesn't mean you've mastered the market, but it does mean you're moving closer to mastery. These flashes of insight are stepping stones, each one bringing you closer to understanding the market in its full complexity.

But don't be fooled into thinking that these moments come often or easily. They are rare, like glimpses of a hidden truth. And just as they appear, they can vanish if you don't make the most of them. The key is to act on them, to integrate the insights into your strategy and continue moving forward.

Once you've experienced your first "aha moment" , the pursuit of the next one becomes part of your journey. Each one builds on the last, deepening your knowledge, sharpening your instincts, and refining your strategy. The mind, now trained to find clarity in rest, becomes your most powerful tool in navigating the market.

The Flow of Rest and Insight

Like water finding its way through cracks in a stone, insight flows when the mind is still. The "aha moment" is that flow, a rush of understanding that breaks through the barriers of doubt, confusion, and overthinking. But to access it, you must first embrace the art of rest.

It's in those moments of quiet, whether it's a walk, a meditation, or simply a deep breath, that the market reveals its secrets to you. This is your edge as a strategist, not just in how hard you work, but in how deeply you rest and allow the mind to process, recover, and eventually, transform your trading. to new heights.

Chapter 18

The Currency of Energy: Being Intentional with Time

In the world of trading, it's easy to think that success is purely a matter of skill, knowledge, and strategy. But beneath these visible components lies something more fundamental, something often overlooked but critical to long-term success, your energy. Energy is the real currency you trade, and how you manage it can either propel you forward or bring you to a standstill. Just as you would manage your financial capital, you must also manage your energy with intention, focus, and care.

Mastering your energy is about more than just physical stamina; it's about being mindful of where and how you spend your time. Time and energy are inextricably linked, spend your time on the wrong activities, and you drain your energy with little to show for it. Spend your time with purpose, and you'll not only protect your energy but multiply its impact, using it to drive the results you desire.

The Energy Equation

Energy is often thought of as something limitless, especially in the high-octane world of trading, where the pressure to perform is constant. There's a sense that you should always be on, always scanning the market, always ready to make the next move. But this mindset is not sustainable, and over time it leads to burnout, fatigue, and a decline in performance. Energy, much like your trading account, is finite. Every action you take, every decision you make, draws from that energy bank.

In trading, you have to be selective about where you allocate your energy, just as you are selective about where you allocate your trades. Successful traders know that energy is a valuable asset, one that must be carefully managed to ensure they stay sharp, focused, and ready for the next opportunity.

Time as a Mirror for Energy

Time and energy share a close relationship, but they are not the same. Time is objective measured in hours, minutes, seconds but energy is subjective, felt in waves of focus, creativity, and motivation. The mistake many traders make is treating time as their only resource, forgetting that without energy, time becomes useless.

You may have 12 hours in a trading day, but if your energy is depleted after five, those remaining hours are wasted. Without energy, you'll find yourself making impulsive decisions, second-guessing your strategies, and losing the ability to think clearly. Your mind becomes cloudy, and the sharpness you once had fades away, replaced by exhaustion and frustration.

This is why it's not just about how much time you have, but how you use it. Being intentional with your time means aligning it with your energy cycles. Every person has natural ebbs and flows in their energy levels throughout the day, and these cycles dictate when you are most productive and focused. The key is to understand your personal rhythm and plan your trading activities accordingly.

Finding Your Power HoursProtecting Your Energy Bank

Your energy, like your capital, is limited. And just as you would never waste your money on a poor investment, you must be careful not to waste your energy on activities that drain you without yielding returns. This means becoming intentional about what you say yes to and learning the power of saying no.

In trading, distractions are everywhere. There's always another chart to analyze, another headline to read, another forum to check. But not every task is worth your time or energy. The more you allow yourself to be pulled in different directions, the more scattered and depleted you become. The master strategist understands this and guards their energy fiercely.

To protect your energy bank, you must learn to filter out the noise and focus on what truly matters. This means setting clear priorities, creating boundaries, and minimizing distractions. It's about becoming laser-focused on the activities that move the

the needle in your trading and letting go of the rest. By doing this, you conserve your energy for the tasks that will bring the most significant returns.

The Power of Intention

Energy follows intention. Where you direct your focus, your energy will flow. This is why being intentional with your time is crucial to maximizing your energy. It's not just about being busy; it's about being purposeful with every action you take.

Before you start your trading day, take a moment to set your intentions. What do you want to accomplish today? What trades are you looking for? What mindset will you bring to the market? By setting clear intentions, you give your energy a target to aim for. You create a sense of direction that prevents you from drifting aimlessly or becoming overwhelmed by the endless stream of information that the market throws at you.

When you operate with intention, you become more focused, more disciplined, and more in control of your energy. You move through your day with purpose, knowing exactly where to allocate your time and attention. And when you combine intention with a deep understanding of your energy rhythms, you unlock a level of productivity and clarity that few traders ever achieve.

The Importance of Recovery

Just as you need to be intentional about how you spend your energy, you also need to be intentional about how you recover it. Energy, once spent, must be replenished, and this requires deliberate recovery practices. Without recovery, you'll find yourself running on empty, with no reserves left to draw from when the market demands your full attention.

Recovery can take many forms, physical rest, mental breaks, or even emotional release. The key is to find what works for you and to make recovery a regular part of your routine. This could be as simple as taking a walk in nature, practicing meditation, or spending time with loved ones. Whatever it is, make sure it's something that truly restores your energy and helps you come back to the market refreshed and recharged.

Energy as a Competitive Edge

In the high-stakes world of trading, every advantage counts. And while most traders focus solely on their strategies, the real edge comes from mastering your energy. When you manage your energy with intention, you stay sharp, focused, and ready to seize opportunities when they arise. You become more resilient in the face of challenges and more consistent in your decision-making.

The traders who burn out, who lose their edge, are the ones who fail to recognize the importance of energy management. They push themselves too hard, spend their time on the wrong activities, and neglect their need for rest and recovery. Over time, their performance suffers, and they find themselves falling behind.

But the master strategist understands that energy is the true currency of success. They know that by managing their energy with care, they can maintain their focus, their discipline, and their drive, even in the most volatile market conditions. And it's this mastery of energy that allows them to stay at the top of their game, year after year.

Becoming a Master of Time and Energy

To become a true master strategist, you must learn to view time and energy as two sides of the same coin. Time without energy is wasted, and energy without time is directionless. But when you align the two, when you use your time with intention and manage your energy with care, you unlock a level of performance that sets you apart from the rest.

Being intentional with your time means understanding when you're at your best and structuring your day around those moments of peak energy. It means guarding your energy fiercely, focusing only on what truly matters, and letting go of the rest. And it means recognizing the importance of recovery, allowing yourself the space to recharge so that you can come back stronger than before.

The market will always be there, always moving, always tempting you to push harder, work longer, and give more. But the true master strategist knows that success isn't about working harder, it's about working smarter. It's about using your time and energy with purpose, intention, and precision. And it's this mastery of energy that will carry you to long-term success, both in trading and in life.

Conclusion:
The Journey of Mastery

Mastery is not a destination. It's a journey one that never truly ends. As you reach the end of this book, you stand at the beginning of a new phase in your development as a strategist, one who views trading not as a race to quick profits but as a long-term pursuit of excellence.

Throughout these chapters, you've learned that strategy is not just about finding the perfect entry or exit; it's about creating a mindset that embraces growth, learning, and adaptation. You've discovered that failure is not a sign of defeat, but a necessary step on the path to mastery. You've explored how discipline, patience, and rest, often overlooked in the fast-paced world of trading, are your silent weapons, sharpening your edge in ways that technical analysis alone cannot.

But the journey does not stop here.

The market is a living, breathing entity, constantly shifting and evolving. To stay ahead, you must evolve with it. The greatest traders understand that they are always students, always learning, and always adjusting. What you do next is just as important as what you've learned so far. The market will continue to test you, and in those moments, you must remind yourself that every challenge, every loss, every victory is a part of your growth.

The key to lasting success lies not just in the strategies you've developed but in your ability to coach yourself, to reflect on your progress, and to continually refine your approach. Like a master strategist on the battlefield, you must remain vigilant, flexible, and ready to adapt to new circumstances. This isn't a game you can win in one move, it's about building a system that can thrive over countless cycles, seasons, and shifts.

You've also learned that the mind is your most valuable asset. Guard it fiercely. Know when to push forward, and when to step back. Understand that true mastery involves moments of rest and reflection, where the greatest insights and "aha moments" are often born. It's not about outworking everyone; it's about outlasting them with a calm, focused mind and a relentless commitment to your long-term goals.

As you move forward, remember that trading is not just a test of skill, it's a test of character. The markets will reveal your strengths, but more importantly, they will expose your weaknesses. Use those moments to grow, to refine, and to evolve into the trader you are destined to become.

The journey of a master strategist is never over, but that's what makes it so powerful. Every step you take is another layer of wisdom, another piece of the puzzle that brings you closer to your true potential. Keep moving forward, keep thinking ahead, and keep playing the long game. The market is your battlefield, and you are now equipped with the mindset, the tools, and the discipline to not just survive, but thrive.

This is your journey. And the best is yet to come.

www.ingramcontent.com/pod-product-compliance
Lightning Source LLC
Chambersburg PA
CBHW052300220526
45471CB00001B/416